43 WINE REGIONS

www.mascotbooks.com

43 Wine Regions

For more information, please contact:
Mascot Books
620 Herndon Parkway #320
Herndon, VA 20170
info@mascotbooks.com

Library of Congress Control Number: 2018902634

CPSIA Code: PRTWP0618A
ISBN-13: 978-1-68401-759-1

Back cover image: Photo by Erica Everhart on location at Stone Tower Winery, Leesburg, Virginia.

Bordeaux image: Photo by Ruth Blanco Biddick on location at Château Lafite Rothschild, Pauillac, France.

Printed in Malaysia

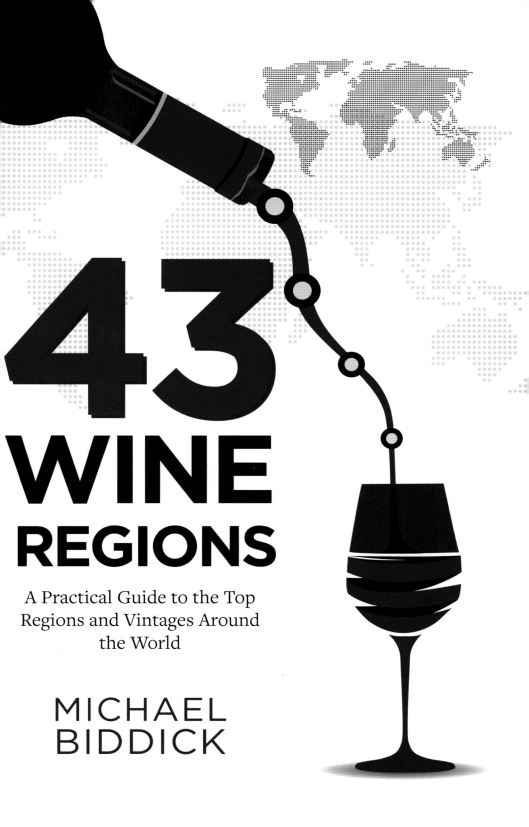

43 WINE REGIONS

A Practical Guide to the Top
Regions and Vintages Around
the World

MICHAEL
BIDDICK

CONTENTS

NEW ZEALAND

SOUTH AFRICA

INTRODUCTION

I was talking with a friend about the final stages of writing this book and he said, "Oh—it's like Moneyball for wine." That was the first time I made that connection, but I did not want to write a heavy hitting book about the process of data analytics and statistics. Researching this book involved a lot of data analysis and number crunching in a yeoman's quest to find the greatest wine-producing regions and recent vintages in the world. But while developing the book, I also traveled to many of the wine-producing regions, met the producers, and learned about their generations of perfected winemaking techniques. I sampled different wines from all over the world and tried a lot of good—and some not-so-good—wines. My research included tasting many unfinished wines still in the barrel to determine how future vintages might develop.

Hundreds of Internet websites debate wine and food pairings, praise the best producers, and dissect nearly every aspect of the juice extracted from grapes all over the world. What many wine industry experts don't like to talk about is the tendency to push many wines to the top of reviewers' lists based on marketing hype. With thousands of wineries from dozens of countries producing wine from a multitude of grapes and blends, everyone is chasing differentiation, accolades from the press, and top scores from wine experts.

Instead of jumping on the bandwagon, I wanted to share my notes to help consumers select wines at restaurants, order bottles online, or shop at their favorite wine shop based on data. I wanted to write something that people could throw in their carry-on bag as they traveled to faraway countries where some of the best wine is produced.

The land, climate, and winemaking traditions in any region will greatly influence the taste and style of the wine. What is the local soil like? How was the weather last year? Do producers age their wine in oak barrels, stainless steel, or maybe concrete? These are all important questions to consider when you are selecting a wine, but you will not see any of that information on a label.

Every wine-growing region has its own detailed quality classification system that can steer you toward superior or value wine, depending on what you need for a particular occasion. Some regions use words like "Reserve" or "Classico" to describe a wine, but those labels may not mean anything in terms of the quality. In certain areas, those declarations have very specific meanings indicating the aging requirements and/or the grapes used in the production of the wine. In other regions, those labels are just marketing words. Some wines state the grapes used on the bottle; others do not. A lot of the requirements and traditions for labeling the bottles a particular way come back to the regions.

I invite you to try the wines produced in these regions and compare notes. I hope that you enjoy your journey as much as I did.

WHY 43?

I never intended to write a book about wine regions. As someone with a background in information technology, I found the task of choosing a wine to be a little too mysterious. Going all in, I started to travel to the places in the world that made wine and studied to become a sommelier. I kept coming back to the tremendous number of variables that were involved in picking a great wine. While I found a few websites that tried to match personal tastes to wine, I thought that there must be a way to crunch the data and provide some generalities on selecting great wine.

Since there are literally thousands of different wines in the world, I thought that focusing on the wine regions might be a good place to start. My idea was that if I knew the wine regions that generally produce the best wine, then I would have a pretty good shot at getting a great bottle. I decided to look at the wines from 2000 onward. In 2015, I started to work on an algorithm that would analyze data related to wine production and generate a report of the best wine regions in the world. The algorithm focused on three distinct sets of data, in addition to a sensory evaluation.

The first group was weather data. Each region has specific rainfall targets, days of sunshine, and temperature targets during the growing season. There are also extreme weather events like hail storms and early or late frost that will have a negative impact on the grapes. For each year, in each region, I collected weather data. This was actually a lot harder than I thought it would be, since each country's weather data existed for a city, but not necessarily a growing region. So, while I was able to use metropolitan weather data as a starting point, I started researching individual vineyards and collecting their sometimes-subjective data on their experiences with weather. It was clear that climate change was having a significant impact on hundreds of years of wine production in most regions in the world. Many producers are struggling to deal with these changes. Aside from temperature change, extreme weather events were also much more significant over the past decade. From fires in California to hail storms in France and heat waves in Chile, climate change is having a major impact on wine growers. Weather generally affects the region and their amount of wine produced, but how about quality? Can wine producers work with grapes grown in less-than-ideal conditions to produce a great wine?

The next data set was consumer feedback. Here, I grouped and input reviews from people that tried wines from these regions. While everyone's taste might be a little different, I thought that normalizing the ratings and reviews from multiple sources would produce some additional reference points to judge the quality of the wine. Aside from the diverse data collection and normalization task, another aspect I considered was when people were drinking the wine. For example, the experience drinking a 2005 Médoc from Bordeaux would be different in 2017, compared to trying it in 2008. For some wines, time matters. Many tasters also provided subjective comments that needed to be translated into numeric scores.

The final dataset was focused on the level of maturity for regional quality standards. These standards set a bar for winemakers to utilize the most marketable names and labels on their wine. My assumption was that most winemakers would strive to achieve these standards through their vinification techniques. Each country and each region have different quality standards for their wine. Some of these regions' quality systems, like the 1855 Bordeaux classification, are based on historical legacy or price points in the market and are not necessarily representative of quality.

I started with 197 wine-growing regions across thirty different countries, from well-known regions within Spain, Italy, and France to more obscure regions within Mexico, China, and Turkey. I created three different tiers (Great, Average, and Inconsistent) based on weighted total points. Please see the Appendix at the back of this book for the complete scores of the wine regions. Based on the margin of error for the datasets and the results, I did not rank the regions in order.

After I created my initial dataset, I blind-tasted the wines to validate my findings. Comparing the results of the data to several blind tastings over a year, I was able to select the greatest wine region in each case when compared to one of the other regions. Within a region, I was generally able to select the better vintages and classifications based on the year produced. There were only a few tweaks needed where I felt that data did not support my evaluation of the quality of the wine. While there were some amazing individual wines from certain countries, I was looking for generalities. For example, the chances of ordering a great wine from the Duna region in Hungary are a lot lower than picking a terrific German wine from Pfalz.

Like many challenges involving big data analytics, so much of the problem is not the tools or the analysis but the quality of the underlying data. With thousands of producers within a growing region, and significant variability in methods, across different years, a lot more data would have been needed—and unfortunately, it does not exist or is not accessible. The lack of uniformity across regions was also a significant challenge to produce common datasets that could be easily compared, but in this case, data can get you eighty percent of the way to discovering great wine.

From the project, I quickly realized that while the data analysis was a great starting point, it could not replace the experience of tasting the wines and evaluating quality. Personal preferences also play an important factor in wine selection, so even though the data may point to a great growing region, a person may not like the style of wine. Wine selection isn't a mystery, but finding great wine is a journey more than a destination.

WINE-GROWING REGIONS

While I now had this data, I encountered two major problems when I decided to write about the wine-growing regions. The first problem was that there is no global standard for how to define a wine region. Each country has ways to designate wine-growing regions and has different levels of geographic granularity. Every part of the world has different practices to break down growing zones based a wide range of criteria. European countries have a more complex structure than newer wine regions in the Americas, New Zealand, Australia, or South Africa.

For example, in the United States, Virginia can be considered a wine-growing region. At the same time, you also could consider each of the seven American Viticultural Areas (AVAs) within Virginia as a region. While dealing with seven growing regions within a geographic area the size of Virginia is manageable, many of the older growing regions in France, Spain, Italy, and others have many more granular designations for wine. In France, for example, there are over 500 Appellation d'Origine Contrôlée (AOCs), and all have distinct soil composition, microclimates, and wine styles. Some of these AOCs are very large and could be considered a region, but some are very small and difficult to justify as a distinct zone. In Bordeaux alone, there are sixty AOCs.

The second problem was that all of the wine producers within a region do not just mix all of their grapes together to produce a common wine from the region. Even in the smaller regions, with strict style and quality controls, there is a tremendous amount of diversity, and generalizations become very hard. When we discuss France, I include Burgundy as a region, but I could have narrowed that to just the Côte-d'Or—but the Côte-d'Or could be divided into the Côte de Beaune and Côte de Nuits. Even if I did that, it could be argued that within each of those regions, I could have further divided the subregions and filled a book with the greatest wines from Morey-Saint-Denis, which is inside the Côte de Beaune. These would have included mostly reds, but some whites across a range of styles defined by unique climate and soils. Even the producers within those microregions produce different wines.

Hopefully, learning more about the regions will inspire you to explore them and learn about the different styles, producers, and wines. This book will ideally stir your first steps into the vineyards and encourage lifelong learning about wine.

WINE QUALITY IN THE REGIONS

Quality standards, like regions, are important to understand in the wine world. With a little information about these frameworks, you can greatly increase your chances of choosing a great bottle of wine.

Within the European Union (EU), there are two basic designations for quality wine. The primary goal of these standards is to ensure that the grapes used for the wines come from a specific place within the EU. The two designations for wine produced within the EU are:

- Protected Designation of Origin (PDO), and
- Protected Geographical Indication (PGI).

PDO requires that one-hundred percent of the grapes must be from the specified region. PGI requires that eighty-five percent of the grapes must be from the specified region. The remaining fifteen percent may come from outside the geographical area so long as they are from the same country.

Where it gets a little confusing is that each country in the EU may translate these designations into their local language. So, in France a PDO is translated to Appellation d'Origine Protégée (AOP). Before these quality designations were created, countries also had their own quality designations that were stricter that the PDO/PGI designation, and these are often still used within the regions. An AOC, as an example, is also automatically considered an AOP (or PDO). The table below shows the terms that may be used on the bottles to indicate that wine is from a specific region.

EU	France	Italy	Spain	Portugal	Austria	Germany
PDO	AOC AOP	DOC DOCG DOP	DO DOCa DOP	IPR DOC	DAC Qualitäts- wein Prädikats- wein	QbA Prädikats- wein
PGI	VDP	IGT	VT	VR	Landwein	Landwein

Table: European Wine Quality Standards on the Label

The term "d'Origin" is also often replaced by the actual name of the place. So, an example of a French wine that meets AOC standards may state "Appellation Bordeaux Contrôlée" on the label. Many countries, especially France, will have stricter controls within their quality standards. A producer within Bordeaux that has a vineyard within the Graves subregion, for example, may state "Appellation Graves Contrôlée," as Graves has a reputation that is superior to general Bordeaux AOC wines.

The standards for many of the country-specific wine regions also go well beyond the regional designation. The region may add production restrictions, aging standards, alcohol level thresholds, and other variables to produce wine that is typical of that area. The strictest quality standards are normally the country-specific designations, which is why many providers have not switched over to the EU terminology.

Outside the EU, the New World wine regions also have quality standards that focus on ensuring that the grapes are grown within the zones specified on the bottle, but they stop there. Generally, New World wine producers have a lot more flexibility in terms of the grapes used, aging time and process, and general vinification methods.

Just because a wine meets a quality standard does not mean that you will like it. At a party, I once served Château-Chalon AOC Vin Jaune. This is a white wine from Savoie in France that is aged for seven years. It has strong flavors of nuts, spices, and baking bread. It was a great example of high-quality wine. No one liked it. I heard a lot of comments like, "Wow, that is interesting," but it was not a hit. So, while the quality standards within the regions can be a guide, you need to determine what your individual tastes are for levels of sweetness, alcohol levels, fruitiness, minerality, and other characteristics. You will discover what you like through experimentation, but with the overwhelming number of wines in the world, start the journey with the regions and remember that wine is personal.

OTHER FACTORS IN GREAT WINE

Leaning about the wine regions is a great start to helping you choose a great wine. There are other factors that you will want to consider.

1. Will you be drinking this wine with a meal? Wine pairs with food, so different wines will enhance (or detract from) certain foods.

2. Do you like wines that express more fruit, or ones that convey more minerals? European wines will generally have more minerality, while New World wines will be fruitier.

3. When are you drinking the wine in relation to the age of the bottle? Some wines are meant to be consumed a year or less after bottling. Others should be aged for ten years or more. In Bordeaux, they say that drinking a wine that is meant to be aged is like killing a baby. Don't be a baby killer.

4.   How much do you want to spend on the bottle? Wines from different regions have different price points, and it is not always because the more expensive bottle is better. Marketing and demand can drive price.

5.   How is the weather when you will be drinking? Rosé and white wines are generally better in summer; deep reds, in winter (unless they are with food).

6.   How was the wine stored? Did the bottle sit in a hot shipping container before getting to the store? Don't leave wine in a hot car after you buy it. Travel and storage conditions will definitely affect the taste of the wine.

7.   Will the wine be served at the correct temperature? An amazing wine too hot or too cold will ruin the experience of great wines.

8.   Do you want just a glass, or a bottle? At a restaurant, I do not recommend ordering non-sparkling wine by the glass, but if you do, how long the bottle has been open will affect the taste of the wine. Usually the lowest quality wines on their menu are also sold by the glass.

9.   How was the weather during the growing season for that vintage of wine? Extreme weather will have a big impact on the grapes and the wine.

10. How consistent is the producer within the region at creating top-quality wines? Even within some of the best wine regions, there is a lot of variety in the quality of the producers.

Knowing the top wine regions is the best place to start; however, keep all of these other factors in mind to get the best experience from wine.

INFOGRAPHIC KEY

Each of the growing regions has a corresponding infographic that includes a ranking of the vintages for a seventeen-year period. Some additional information on the climate, geography, primary grapes, and important subregions are also included here.

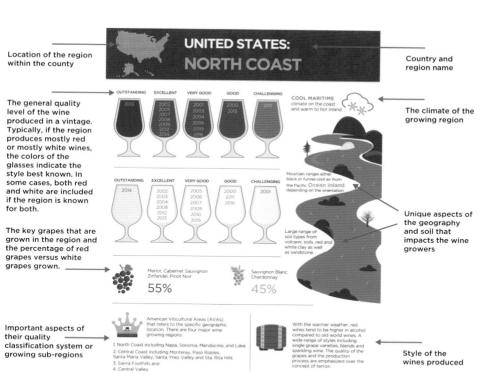

Location of the region within the county

UNITED STATES:
NORTH COAST

Country and region name

The general quality level of the wine produced in a vintage. Typically, if the region produces mostly red or mostly white wines, the colors of the glasses indicate the style best known. In some cases, both red and white are included if the region is known for both.

OUTSTANDING	EXCELLENT	VERY GOOD	GOOD	CHALLENGING
2013	2002 2005 2007 2008 2009 2012 2014	2001 2003 2004 2006 2010 2016	2000 2015	2011

COOL MARITIME climate on the coast and warm to hot inland.

The climate of the growing region

OUTSTANDING	EXCELLENT	VERY GOOD	GOOD	CHALLENGING
2014	2002 2003 2004 2008 2012 2013	2005 2006 2007 2009 2010 2015	2000 2011 2016	2001

Mountain ranges either black or funnel cool air from the Pacific Ocean inland depending on the orientation.

The key grapes that are grown in the region and the percentage of red grapes versus white grapes grown.

Large range of soil types from volcanic soils, red and white clay as well as sandstone.

Unique aspects of the geography and soil that impacts the wine growers

Merlot, Cabernet Sauvignon Zinfandel, Pinot Noir
55%

Sauvignon Blanc Chardonnay
45%

Important aspects of their quality classification system or growing sub-regions

American Viticultural Areas (AVAs) that refers to the specific geographic location. There are four major wine growing regions:

1. North Coast including Napa, Sonoma, Mendocino, and Lake.
2. Central Coast including Monterey, Paso Robles, Santa Maria Valley, Santa Ynez Valley and Sta. Rita Hills
3. Sierra Foothills and
4. Central Valley

With the warmer weather, red wines tend to be higher in alcohol compared to old world wines. A wide range of styles including single grape varieties, blends and sparkling wine. The quality of the grapes and the production process are emphasized over the concept of terroir.

Style of the wines produced

FRANCE

Wine is woven more deeply into the culture of the French people than any other part of the world. Thirteen major growing areas dot the French landscape throughout the country. These include icons like Bordeaux and Burgundy as well as lesser-known regions in Corsica, Jura, and Languedoc-Roussillon. The vastness and history of the French wine market may be daunting, but getting to know these regions is a must for any wine lover.

To drink French wine, you must understand the regions first. In France, people will say, "I feel like drinking a St.-Joseph tonight." They will not say, "how about a Syrah?" While it may be extra work to enjoy French wines, it will be worth your time. From rich reds to sweet whites, the diversity and complexity of France's wine regions can please every taste. The regions across France represent the full spectrum of wines available in the world and will satisfy most drinkers, once they find the one that best suits their palate. As the top-producing wine region in the world in terms of quantity, France's approach to winemaking techniques, creating blends, and the importance of the land have been emulated throughout the world.

Buying a bottle of French wine without any knowledge is a throw of the dice. While most people have the basic understanding that a Merlot grape produces a red wine, the French, with the exception of the Alsace region, do not place grape names on the bottle labels. Sometimes, you will find an importer's label that may explain the wine, including the grapes, on the back of the bottle, but it is not standard practice. Instead, French wine producers indicate the name of the winemaker and the region prominently on the label.

The lack of grape names of the bottles of French wine is intentional. In France, wine is all about a concept called "terroir," which does not translate exactly into English. Literally meaning "dirt," "terroir" is an expression of place in the wine. The place reflects century-old limestone in the soil, rolling hills protecting vines from harsh weather, or a specific sunny spot on a hill. These are some of the factors that represent terroir, and it is the most important concept to understand about French wine.

In the early 1900s, counterfeiters took advantage of France's marketing success and wine quality by selling low-quality fermented grape juice in France and abroad, labeled as some of the regions' top producers. To address this problem and protect the integrity of terroir, in the mid-1930s, the French government instituted a quality control labeling system called "Appellation d'Origine Contrôlée" (AOC). To label wine from the growing region, the wine producers needed to follow certain requirements. These included using grapes from defined standard geographic boundaries, rules around which specific grape varieties can be used in the wine, aging requirements, production levels, and other standards unique to the wine produced in that growing region. The AOC label is an indicator of the terroir in wine, and a very important item to read on French wine labels. Wine producers in France may choose not to conform to AOC standards and still produce great wine, but they are not able to use the AOC label.

The climate, soils and grape varieties are quite diverse in France. In the north, the grapes in Champagne, Alsace and Burgundy may struggle to ripen and need to survive through hail storms, cold winds and early spring frost. In the south, scorching heat and long dry summers can cause photosynthesis to stop as temperatures soar. Outside of the extremes, however, France's wine-growing regions benefit from a balanced climate that is well suited to the grapes and the soil. Chardonnay is the most common white grape planted for wine. While best known in Burgundy, it makes up a third of all plantings in Champagne and even more in Languedoc-Roussillon. Merlot is the most prominent red variety, followed by Cabernet Sauvignon and Cabernet Franc. Hundreds of other varieties exist, especially in the south.

While not exclusive to France, biodynamic agriculture is becoming more common, especially among the higher quality producers. This approach to winemaking is not only about reducing or eliminating chemical fertilization, pesticides and herbicides, but about keeping the vines and the land in balance with nature. Biodynamic winemaking employs herbal and mineral solutions like compost additives, sprays in the field and the use of a lunar-based planting calendar. One producer in southwest France first told me about Leaf Days, Flower Days, Fruit Days and Root Days and how the position of the moon governs the planting (and even the wine tasting) schedule. While this all seemed a little odd to me, the very first farmers relied on the lunar cycles for planting and maintenance, so it is not a new concept. For a biodynamic winegrower, the interrelation of soils, plants and animals are viewed as a system where self-nutrition without outside intervention is desirable. The organization Demeter is the control and certification body for biodynamic agriculture in France and while some producers will use organic and biodynamic approaches, many may choose not to obtain certification because of the significant costs involved. Some producers go beyond biodynamic winemaking and also avoid adding sulfites (a preservative) to their wine, taking the risk that their wines age poorly. These are called Natural Wines and they are increasingly trendy in France, Italy, Spain and the United States.

FRANCE:
BURGUNDY

OUTSTANDING	EXCELLENT	VERY GOOD	GOOD
2005 2015	2002 2009 2010 2012 2014 2016	2001 2003 2006 2008	2000 2004 2007 2011 2013

Continental climate with **ROLLING HILLS.**

EXCELLENT	VERY GOOD	GOOD	CHALLENGING
2005 2006 2010 2011 2015	2007 2008 2009 2012 2013 2014	2000 2001 2002 2003 2016	2004

Chalk, calcareous clay, limestone, and marl.

 Pinot Noir
65%

 Chardonnay
35%

Terroir is the most important classification aspect. There are four levels of quality classifications: Grand Cru, Premier Cru, Village Wines and Regional Appellation.

The four major regions are Chablis, Côte d'Or, Côte Chalonnaise, and Mâconnais. Within the Côte d'Or, Côte de Beaune is widely recognized for white wines and Côte de Nuits for their red wines.

Chablis uses 100% Chardonnay with oak and malolactic fermentation. Côte d'Or is known for significant use of new French oak for both the red and white wines. Côte Chalonnaise and Mâconnais produce both reds and whites, but rarely use oak, aside from Pouilly-Fuissé.

This out-of-the-way corner of northeastern France consistently produces some of the best red and white wines in the world. Here you will find a vast range of producers, including some of the most sought-after and collectible vintages, alongside outstanding (yet affordable) bottles. Most Burgundy reds are produced using only one hundred percent Pinot Noir, while most whites are produced using only one hundred percent Chardonnay.

However, Burgundy is not as much about the grapes as it is the story of the soil and climate that compose the diverse region. If there is one region in France that truly embodies terroir, it would be Burgundy. Burgundy is known for the unique qualities that grapes draw from the environment and the land. The limestone and marl soil, combined with the climate of Burgundy, are a perfect match for the Chardonnay and Pinot Noir grapes.

While Burgundy does not go as far as naming each individual grapevine, they come closer than any other wine region. A "climat," which comes from the French word for "climate," is a unique parcel of vines, carefully marked and named for centuries. A climat has its own history and qualities based on specific geographic and environmental factors.

Within Burgundy, there is a quality hierarchy which is mostly based on terroir: Grand Cru, Premier Cru, village wines, and regional wines. In the Côte-d'Or, there are twenty-four Grand Cru wines. These designations will usually translate to higher prices; however, the quality lines can be blurry between the different quality tiers. Generally, a Premier Cru zone will have the right environment, grapes, and soil to produce a wine that is better than a village wine. The climate is also highly variable, so you will find a lot of differences from year to year in terms of the quality, even in the Cru wines.

Recommend drinking bottles five to seven or more years after the bottle date.

FRANCE:
BORDEAUX

OUTSTANDING	EXCELLENT	VERY GOOD	GOOD	CHALLENGING
2005 2009 2010 2016	2000 2003 2014 2015	2001 2004 2006 2008 2011 2012	2002 2007	2013

Maritime climate
RAIN & FROST
common.

Gravel on the Left Bank -
Medoc and Graves.

Merlot
Cabernet Sauvignon
Cabernet Franc

80%

Sauvignon Blanc
Semillion

20%

Limestone
and clay on the
Right Bank -
**Saint-Emilion
and Pomerol.**

Classifications

Key Left Bank AOCs:
Medoc, Saint-Estephe, Pauillac,
Saint-Julien, Margaux, Graves,
Pessac-Léognan, Sauternes.

Key Right Bank AOCs:
Saint-Emilion, Pomerol, Fronsac, Blaye,
Saint-Foy Bordeaux, Bourg

Blends, typically aged in
new French oak. Most red wines
should be aged for up to ten years
before drinking.

One of the most important things to know about Bordeaux wines is that they are a blend of grape varieties. The red Bordeaux blend is one of the most copied recipes around the world, including Cabernet Sauvignon, Merlot, and Cabernet Franc. Red Bordeaux wines are elegantly styled with firm tannin levels. Tannins are naturally occurring compounds that add both bitterness and astringency to most red wines. These same tannins also aid in the complexity that develops a softness as red wines age. The tannins in Bordeaux reds can be very strong and not pleasant to drink when the wine is young. Over time, the tannins soften, allowing the other flavors to develop. This is why it is best to drink older Bordeaux red vintages.

While most known for dry red wines which comprise about ninety percent of total production, Bordeaux has thirty-eight subregions with fifty-seven different AOCs, including some outstanding dry white and sweet varieties. Saint-Émilion, about forty minutes east of the city of Bordeaux, is within the Bordeaux growing region and also has its own classification system and outstanding vintages.

There are two major areas in Bordeaux: the left bank and the right bank. The names are derived from the location of each area in relation to the Gironde estuary. You should know that on the left bank, Cabernet Sauvignon dominates the blend, whereas Merlot dominates the right bank. Like Burgundy, the climate is highly variable, and weather plays an important part of the quality in the vintages. I was standing in a vineyard in Margaux, rain pouring down on my head and dark storm clouds overhead. The vineyard across the street, only thirty yards (or ninety feet) away, was dry and sunny.

Recommend drinking bottles four to six or more years after the bottle date.

FRANCE:
CHAMPAGNE

OUTSTANDING	EXCELLENT	VERY GOOD	GOOD	CHALLENGING
2002 2012	2005 2008 2013 2015	2004 2006 2007 2009 2011	2003 2010 2014 2016	2000 2001

Cool continental climate with **NO NATURAL PROTECTION** from the Atlantic Ocean. Unpredictable weather.

Limestone and chalk.

 Pinot Noir
Pinot Meunier
50%

 Chardonnay
50%

Classifications

Non-vintage (NV) champagne is aged for at least 15 months. Vintage champagne is aged a minimum of 36 months, all in the bottle before it is sold.

Three main styles: Blanc de Blancs (100% Chardonnay), Blanc de Noirs (Pinot Noir and Pinot Meunier), and Rosé. Producers may create a Cuvée Prestige or Tête de Cuvée as the top-end bottling. Most champagne is a blend of grapes.

There is only one Champagne. Everything else is sparkling wine. Champagne 145 kilometers (ninety miles) east of Paris and is cool, wet, and rainy. The chalky limestone soil in Champagne is a key element to what makes the region—and the sparkling wines—unique. The climate and soil are ideal for Champagne's grape varieties: Pinot Noir, Pinot Meunier, and Chardonnay. There are five very distinct regions in Champagne with different climates and different soils. Most of the best Grand Cru Champagnes come from Montagne de Reims and Côte des Blancs near the town of Épernay.

When purchasing Champagne, you will be confronted with vintage and non-vintage varieties. Non-vintage Champagne uses grapes from different years and must be aged for at least fifteen months before sale. Vintage Champagne must contain grapes mostly from the vintage year on the label and must be stored for at least three years before bringing them to market. Nearly all quality vintage Champagnes far exceed the minimum aging requirements, and you may find vintage Champagnes ten or fifteen years old that have just been released.

The other key element to understand is the sweetness level of Champagne. The most popular type of Champagne is Brut. In actuality, there are six levels of Champagne sweetness based on the percentage of natural residual sugar that remains in the bottle after fermentation.

Brut Nature: 0-0.3 percent residual sugar
Extra Brut: 0-0.6 percent residual sugar
Brut: 0-1.2 percent residual sugar
Extra Sec: 1.2-1.7 percent residual sugar
Sec: 1.7-3.2 percent residual sugar
Demi-Sec: 3.2-5 percent residual sugar
Doux: 5+ percent residual sugar

While it is fun to open Champagne with a loud pop, ideally it should make no sound when you open the bottle, as you will want to preserve all of the bubbles in the bottle to drink, instead of letting them escape when pulling the cork.

Recommend drinking bottles six months to three years after the bottle date.

FRANCE:
LOIRE VALLEY

EXCELLENT	VERY GOOD	GOOD	CHALLENGING
2002	2000	2008	2006
2003	2001	2012	2011
2005	2004		2013
2009	2007		
2014	2010		
2016	2015		

COOL AND WET MARITIME CLIMATE off the Atlantic coast to the west and shifting to less maritime influence to the east.

Gravel and sand on top of granite and schist in the west, and soft limestone and Kimmeridgian clay in the east.

Cabernet Franc (Anjou-Saumur, Touraine)

Pinot Noir (Central Vineyards)

25%

Muscadet/Melon de Bourgogne (Pays Nantais)

Sauvignon Blanc (Central Vineyards)

Chenin Blanc (Anjou-Saumur, Touraine)

75%

Classifications

Several significant sub-regions: Pays Nantais, Anjou-Saumur, Touraine, and Sancerre. About 70 AOC classifications exist within the Loire Valley.

The most diverse wine region in France. Western regions use Sur Lie aging. Dessert wine, dry white, sparkling wine, and rosé are all very common. Bourgueil and Chinon (both in Touraine) are the best examples of dry red wines.

White wines and light reds flow with abundance in the Loire Valley. In this region of western France, vineyards blanket a vast area of more than 273 kilometers (270 miles). Such a large region includes diverse terroir, making it difficult to generalize. Nevertheless, more than 4,000 wineries thrive here across several major regions from east to west: Pays Nantais, Anjou, Layon, Saumur, Touraine, and Sancerre.

On the Atlantic coast, the Pays Nantais' dry white wines are often aged for an extended period of time on the dead yeast cells, called "lees." Muscadet is the primary grape here, and on the label, you will often see the words "Sur Lie" to indicate extended aging on the lees. This style adds a sourdough bread flavor to the wine that balances the wine's acidity.

Rosé wines dominate Anjou, where the Grolleau grape is mostly used. These wines may be sweet or dry with several internationally-known AOCs producing consistently high-quality varieties.

Next to Anjou, Layon is best known for sweet white wines made from Chenin Blanc grapes, often affected by botrytis. Botrytis is a beneficial form of a fungus that intensifies the sweetness of the grapes. It develops in cool, moist environments after the grapes ripen on the vine.

Saumur is the Loire's sparkling wine region, producing a range of white and rosé fizzy wines from a variety of grapes. The term "Fines Bulles" is used to describe any sparkling wine in the Loire.

The Loire's best reds come from Touraine. Chinon and Bourgueil are the best examples of full-bodied reds produced from Cabernet Franc that can be aged or consumed shortly after release.

Sancerre produces dry white wines from Sauvignon Blanc with a high degree of minerality from their unique soils found in the region.

Recommend drinking bottles one to two years after the bottle date.

FRANCE:
RHÔNE VALLEY

OUTSTANDING	EXCELLENT	VERY GOOD	GOOD	CHALLENGING
2005	2000	2004	2008	2002
2007	2001	2011	2014	
2009	2003	2012		
2010	2005	2013		
	2006	2016		
	2015			

Continental climate moderated by the Rhône River. Mistral **WINDS WARM** and dry the area.

Syrah
Grenache
Mourvèdre

85%

Viognier
Marsanne
Roussane

15%

Granite and schist soil in the north.

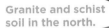

Classifications

The Rhône Valley is split into a Northern and Southern region. Notable Northern appellations include Côte-Rôtie, Condrieu, Saint-Joseph, Crozes-Hermitage, Hermitage, and Cornas. The notable Southern region includes Châteauneuf-du-Pape, Tavel, Gigondas, and Vacqueyras.

Most wine is aged in oak. Single varietals are more typical, especially in the Northern region where reds are 100% Syrah.

Some white grapes are blended with the red.

While there is a single Rhône Valley region that follows the Rhône River, the north and south are quite different. Separating the north and south is a large area of farmland where orchards, olive trees, and other plantings dot the landscape, but no grape vines are grown.

The Northern Rhône wine is only about five percent of the Valley's total production, but the Northern Rhône's signature red Syrah has become the international standard. Appellations like St.-Joseph, Hermitage, Crozes-Hermitage, and Cornas all produce a distinctive one hundred percent Syrah red that varies based on the soils and microclimates of the AOCs. The Northern Rhône also produces a small amount of white wines from Viognier, Marsanne, and Roussanne grapes that are full-bodied and dry with floral notes. The best white wines from the region will be found in Condrieu and Château-Grillet. The most southern of the Northern Rhône AOC Crus, Saint-Péray, produces a very tasty sparkling wine.

In the southern Rhône Valley, you'll find the other ninety-five percent of the region's wines. The king of the south is Châteauneuf-du-Pape, with its dominant red Grenache, Syrah, Mourvèdre (GSM) blend. Châteauneuf-du-Pape wines will also improve dramatically with age and the softening of the tannins. The Gigondas and Vacqueyras are two other powerhouse appellations in the south. The best rosé in France can be found in Tavel, made from the Grenache grape. These distinctive wines are extremely well-structured and possess tannins not found in rosé wines from the Loire and Provence.

Beyond the defined Cru AOCs, the Côtes du Rhône and Côtes du Rhône Village AOCs make up seventy-five percent of the Rhône Valley wines and will be less expensive than the Cru AOCs, but also of very high quality.

Recommend drinking bottles three to seven years after the bottle date.

FRANCE:
ALSACE

EXCELLENT	VERY GOOD	GOOD	CHALLENGING
2001	2000	2006	2003
2002	2004	2011	
2005	2008	2013	
2007	2009	2014	
2010	2015		
2012	2016		

Cool, continental northern climate. The **RAIN SHADOW** from the Vosges mountains produces **DRY AND SUNNY SUMMERS.**

Highly diverse soil types including limestone, marl, granite, clay and schist.

Pinot Noir

10%

Riesling, Gewurtzraminer, Muscat, Pinot Gris

90%

Classifications

There are 51 Alsace Grand Cru vineyards that are allowed to plant only white grapes. A sparkling Crêmant d'Alsace is also produced from a blend of grapes.

Unlike the other regions in France, wines are labeled with the single grape variety used. The sunnier weather and drier climate can produce wines with higher alcohol content and fuller body.

Unlike other parts of France, Alsace is the only entire region in France where you will see specific grapes listed on the bottle, since the region has flipped between France and German control over the centuries. Situated among the Vosges Mountains and west of the Rhine River, Alsace has over a dozen distinct types of soil that snake through the northeast corner of France's map. The climate is dry; the hills, steep; and the scenery, striking.

Riesling, Gewurztraminer, Pinot Gris, and Muscat reign here across fifty-three AOCs. Fifty-one of these AOCs are Grand Cru, but in terms of production only four percent of the wine produced in Alsace is Grand Cru. Eighty percent of the wines are made from a single grape variety, and Riesling dominates. Stylistically, these are dry wines with enough minerality and complexity to drink alone or pair with food. There are some blends, but there are only seven grapes authorized for the Alsace AOC. In addition to the four above, Pinot Noir, Sylvaner, and Pinot Blanc are produced or used in blends.

There are some excellent sparkling wines in Alsace too. These are labeled "Crémant d'Alsace." These wines are hand-picked and produced using the traditional method where the second fermentation, which gives the wine its bubbles, occurs inside the bottle. There is a minimum aging period of nine months on the lees, and then a year in the bottle, before they may be released.

Two sweet wine varieties also exist in Alsace: Selection de Grains Nobles are produced from the four primary grapes (Riesling, Gewurztraminer, Pinot Gris, and Muscat) that are affected by botrytis. Vendage Tardive are late-harvest grapes that remain on the vine until they start to dehydrate.

Recommend drinking bottles six months to three years after the bottle date.

FRANCE:
PROVENCE

OUTSTANDING	EXCELLENT	VERY GOOD	GOOD	CHALLENGING
2007 2015	2000 2009 2014 2016	2001 2003 2006 2008 2011	2004 2005 2010 2012 2013	2002

MEDITERRANEAN CLIMATE with variability depending on the topography and influence of the sea and mistral winds.

Limestone in the **Northwest and crystalline** in the Southeast.

Grenache Noir
Syrah
Mourvedre
Carignan

50%

Clairette
Marsanne
Roussanne
Grenache Blanc

50%

Classifications

Côtes de Provence and Coteaux d'Aix en Provence are the largest AOCs. Almost 90% of the production in Provence is rosé. Cassis produces amazing quality white wines and Bandol top quality reds. Les Beaux de Provence is known for organic and a diverse selection of biodynamic wines.

A wide variety of sweet to dry rosés exist across Provence. Some AOCs specialize in the small production crisp whites and bold red wines as well.

Provence is rosé country. Nearly ninety percent of the region's production consists of rosé, and it is the only region in the world that focuses so much attention on the pink wine. There are four different geographic areas within Provence, and each has a different style of production. Sainte-Victoire, Fréjus, La Londe, and Pierrefeu are all within the Côtes de Provence. These wines have more strict production standards and are notably crisp and fresh. They often show notes of berry, citrus, and spice.

Most of these rosé wines are blends of Grenache, Mourvèdre, Cinsault, Tibouren, and Syrah. The signature aroma and delicate color or Provence's rosés are a result of the direct press production process. As the winemakers gently press the grapes and release their juice, the contact with the skins and tannins are minimized. This preserves the aromas of the fruit and also reduces the color in the wine to produce the signature pink rosé.

Aside from rosé, thirty-six other varieties emerge from this region in the south of France. The AOCs of Bandol and Cassis consistently produce excellent wines. Bandol produces age-worthy, intense reds with bold tannins. Cassis, on the other hand, finds success in its white wines. Varieties such as Clairette, Ugni Blanc, and Marsanne ripen well in one of the warmest regions in France and provide a lot of consistency across vintages.

Les Baux-de-Provence is the largest producer of organic and biodynamic wines in the region. Unlike the other regions, red wines are most prominent here crafted from Grenache, Syrah, and Mourvèdre. While oak is not mandated, the wines must age for at least a year before release.

Recommend drinking bottles upon release.

ITALY

The Greeks called Italy "Oenotria" (the land of wine). The Romans had a god of wine, Bacchus. Catholicism elevated wine as part of the sacrament. This is Italy. Centuries ago, owning a vineyard in Italy was a sign of power and prestige. Today, as the second top-producing wine region in the world, Italy's labyrinth of grapevines now spans the entire country across twenty distinctive growing regions. From the Piedmont in the north, to Sicily in the south, while trekking through the countryside, it would be rare not to see a plot of land growing grapes. From the large-scale producers to backyard hobbyists, Italy loves wine.

Like most things in Italy, wine labels lack conformity. Exploring a bottle, you may see the names of the grapes, sometimes producers, maybe regions, or just a brand name. You might find all those things. While several labeling approaches exist in Italy, many winemakers take liberty in how to mark their bottles, so unless you know what you are looking for, it can be very hard to select Italian wine simply by glancing at the bottle. With Italy's unique grapes, you will not find many common international varieties such as Merlot, Cabernet Sauvignon, or Malbec. Instead, you will find less familiar names like "Sangiovese" and "Nebbiolo," among others.

With its warm summers and strong red wines, Italy also tends to age wines a bit longer before they reach market than other regions do. You may find some good values in older vintages where the tannins have softened and more of the fruit has developed while aging in the bottle.

Italy's wine quality system developed about thirty years after France's. In Italy, there are four levels of quality classifications, from lowest to highest:

- Vino da Tavola (VDT)
- Indicazione Geografica Tipica (IGT)
- Denominazione di Origine, Denominazione di Origine Controllata (DOC) and
- Denominazione di Origine Controllata e Garantita (DOCG).

DOCG labeled wines are analyzed and taste-tasted by Italian government-licensed personnel before being bottled. Once they are bottled, DOC and DOCG wine bottles are tagged with a government seal across the cap or cork, indicating the word "Garantita" (guarantee). Italy's standards, like those of France, mandate alcohol levels, production standards, yields, percentages of grapes that may be used, and aging—all factors that impact the quality of the wine.

Are DOCG wines the best? Not necessarily. However, they have followed additional steps which can lead to a higher quality and more consistent wine. The strict requirements tend to increase the prices, given the additional cost involved with production and conformance.

Italy uses other terms like "Classico," "Riserva," and "Superiore" to describe their wines. Classico is a designation for wines produced using traditional methods in the region. Riserva wines have been aged at least two years longer than the requirement for the wine style. Both terms—Classico and Riserva—may be used together. For example, Chianti Classico must have a minimum alcohol level of at least twelve percent with a minimum of seven months aging in oak, while Chianti Classico Riserva must be aged for at least twenty-four months at the winery and have a minimum alcohol level of at least 12.5 percent. Superiore wines can be produced only from grapes cultivated in a specific geographic region.

Italy has twenty different wine producing regions, and each region has a diverse range of styles and grapes. While over 400 grapes are permitted in Italian wines, researchers have found over 2,000 varieties and sub varieties in the country, with Sangiovese and Trebbiano leading the pack.

With so much variety, many enthusiasts are easily lost when it comes to Italian wines. I have found that the best approach is to focus on a specific region and style or type of wine and then slowly expand from there. Especially in the more popular regions like Piedmont, Veneto and Tuscany, a wide range of price points exist so it is worth getting to know the regions and ultimately the producers in those regions to choose the right bottle.

ITALY:
PIEDMONT

OUTSTANDING	EXCELLENT	VERY GOOD	GOOD	CHALLENGING
2004 2010 2016	2001 2006 2007 2008 2015	2000 2011 2012 2013 2014	2005 2009	2002 2003

Continental climate **PROTECTION FROM THE ALPS CREATING A RAIN SHADOW EFFECT.**

65%

Nebbiolo
Barbera
Dolcetto
Brachetto

35%

Moscato
Cortese
Arneis

Limestone and sandstone soil.

Classifications

Barolo and Barbaresco are the two best known areas. There are 17 DOCGs and 42 DOCs in the Piedmont, more than any other region in Italy. The reds consistently receive most of the attention locally and internationally.

Barolo and Barbaresco use 100% Nebbiolo. Barolo requires 38 months aging, with at least 18 months in oak. Barbaresco requires 24 months of aging, with at least 9 months in oak. Moscato d'Asti-Asti (white) and Brachetto d'Acqui (red) produce sparkling sweeter wines. Gavi produces a dry white wine, using the Cortese grape.

Piedmont produces more DOCGs (seventeen) and DOCs (forty-two) than any other region in Italy. Nationally, while the Piedmont region ranks sixth in wine production volume, they are number one in Italian quality. Some of the best names within the DOCGs are Barolo, Barbaresco, and Asti.

Both Barolo and Barbaresco grow one hundred percent Nebbiolo, but they are quite different wines. Barolo is powerful and complex, while Barbaresco is lighter and more refined. Barolo wines, like Bordeaux reds, are best aged for at least ten years before drinking them as they have very strong tannins. There is also a Barolo Riserva that requires at least five years of aging before release, with eighteen months in oak. Barbaresco wines are fresher than Barolo vintages and do not require as much aging before drinking. They also have a Riserva wine that requires four years of aging before release.

Elsewhere in Piedmont, you will also find a lot of wines using the Barbera grape, as it is the most widely planted varietal in Piedmont. With both high alcohol and high acidity, only a few producers in the Piedmont use Barbera solely, preferring to blend it with other grapes in the region. Nizza wines—the newest DOCG—are the best expression of Barbera.

Piedmont also produces some white wines from a half dozen grapes, but the best-known whites are the sparkling Spumante from Asti and Moscato d'Asti. These are one hundred percent Moscato-based wines and come in a fully sparkling and fizzy version. These wines tend to be sweeter and lower in alcohol than other sparkling wine regions, but in 2017 wine makers in the region started producing dryer versions to meet the market demand for less sweet sparkling wines.

Recommend drinking bottles four to six or more years after the bottle date.

ITALY:
TUSCANY

OUTSTANDING	EXCELLENT	VERY GOOD	GOOD	CHALLENGING
2006 2010	2000 2001 2004 2007 2015 2016	2003 2005 2008 2009 2011 2013	2012 2014	2002

Continental climate, with **SOME MARITIME INFLUENCE** nearer the coast.

   Sangiovese

  Vernaccia

80%

20%

Lower soil quality and **PRODUCTION LEVELS.**

Classifications

Tuscany has 11 DOCGs and 41 DOCs. A separate classification of wine called "Super Tuscans" may also be DOC or DOCG wines, but are not recognized within the Italian wine classification system.

The dry red wines including Brunello di Montalcino, Chicanti, and Chianti Classico are best.

Brunello di Montalcino must be aged two years in wood and four months in bottle before sale. Producers use both very large barrels and smaller barrels for aging.

Tuscany's rolling hills and sun-kissed countryside are perhaps as iconic as its red wines. Tuscany has eleven DOCGs including Chianti, Chianti Classico, and Brunello di Montalcino. Additionally, it has the second most DOCs (forty-one) in Italy.

The most common of Tuscany's grapes is Sangiovese, which is the primary grape in Chianti and must comprise at least seventy-five percent of the wine. The Chianti DOCG has seven subregions, and these may be labeled with the subregion at the preference of the producer. Chianti Rufina is the most renowned of the seven. Chianti also has a Superiore DOCG classification that indicates that the wine was aged an additional two years and three months. These wines typically have the term "Riserva" on the label.

What makes Tuscany unique within Italy, though, is the Super Tuscan wines that are produced outside the DOCG and DOC standards. Since these producers use unauthorized grapes (like Merlot and Cabernet Sauvignon) and non-traditional vinification methods (like small new oak barrels for aging), they are not able to meet DOC or DOCG standards. Often, however, the international market has created a high demand for these Super Tuscans, so the prices may be higher than DOCG wines in the region. In the 1970s, some producers felt that the system's restrictions, developed a decade earlier, were far too rigid. So, the concept of a high-quality wine called "Super Tuscan" that did not follow the wine quality requirements established for the region was born. Most (but not all) Super Tuscans are blends of multiple grapes. Because you will not see the name "Super Tuscan" on the bottle, finding them can be tricky. Some examples of the approximately seventy-five Super Tuscans include Sassicaia, Magari, and Il Bosco.

Recommend drinking bottles three to five or more years after the bottle date.

ITALY:
FRIULI-VENEZIA GIULIA

OUTSTANDING	EXCELLENT	VERY GOOD	GOOD	CHALLENGING
2009 2013	2006 2007 2008 2011 2012	2004 2005 2015 2016	2000 2001 2003 2010	2002 2014

CONTINENTAL CLIMATE. COOL AND RAINY.

GRAVEL SOIL AND CALCAREOUS marl in Collio and Colli Orientali.

Merlot
Refosco

10%

Friulano
Pinot Grigio

90%

Classifications

Friuli has 4 DOCGs and 12 DOCs. The top regions are Friuli Grave, Colli Orientali del Friuli, Collio, and Carso.

The best white wines in Italy. Oak aging is not common among whites.

Friuli-Venezia Giulia (Friuli) is one of Italy's white wine stars. Relying on Pinot Grigio and Friulano for dry whites and sparkling wines, vineyards grow alongside orchards and other agriculture in this cool and rainy region. The region has four DOCGs and twelve DOCs, and about sixty percent of production consists of white wines.

Throughout the region, small-scale wine-makers rely on other local grape varieties to create high-ranking wines in eastern Friuli and produce a long list of small-batch aromatic wines. Friuli is a region that lacks some confidence in its wine production, having undergone a lot of changes over the years. Many producers are adjusting their wines to market tastes, which can create an identity crisis for the region.

If you are looking for fresh white wine, though, Friuli is the best. Some of the great producers are found in two subregions that lie on the border of Slovenia: Friuli Colli Orientali DOC and Collio Goriziano DOC, where a wide range of styles and wines are produced. Here, as in other parts of Friuli, the grapes are placed in a press and then moved into stainless steel vats at controlled temperatures. Winemakers then initiate malolactic fermentation. In this process, the tart-tasting malic acid, naturally occurring in grapes, is converted to softer-tasting lactic acid, so the wines are richer and more buttery tasting. This process produces Italy's signature Pinot Grigio dry, white wine.

Ramandolo, a sweet white, was the first to reach the DOCG ranking. Ramandolo is made from a white but very tannic grape with subtle aroma called Verduzzo that is picked very late in the season and unique to Friuli. Colli Orientali del Friuli Picolit, an aromatic amber wine, followed, and the newest additions to the DOCG category are Lison and Rosazzo.

Recommend drinking bottles upon release.

ITALY:
VENETO

OUTSTANDING	EXCELLENT	VERY GOOD	GOOD	CHALLENGING
2015	2004 2007 2009 2010 2013	2003 2006 2008 2012 2016	2000 2001 2005 2011	2002 2014

Continental climate with a **WARMER MARITIME** climate near the coast.

Gravel, stony soils are well-drained and rich in minerals.

Corvinia Rondinella

45%

Garganega Glera (Prosecco)

55%

Classifications

Veneto is the 8th largest region by volume, but is a top-quality producer. Veneto has 29 DOCs and 14 DOCGs.

Soave Classico indicates that the grapes come from selected vineyards that are considered to be the best.

Venice represents the epicenter of Veneto, this northern Italian wine region. Veneto has fourteen DOCGs and twenty-nine DOCs. Two-thirds of Veneto's wine production is white, and a lot of that is sparkling wine.

If Veneto has a signature grape, it would be the Glera. Known internationally in Prosecco, the Glera grape creates semi-sparkling wines that are recognized around the world. Unlike Champagne, Prosecco DOC has no aging requirements and is typically produced using a tank method. Creation of the bubbles is done in a large tank, in contrast to Champagne and other traditional method processes where the second fermentation happens in each individual bottle. The production method can produce a yeasty flavor in the drink and the bubbles may not last as long in the glass as compared to Champagne. The faster time and bulk production significantly reduces the cost, which is why you see Prosecco a lot more on restaurant and bar menus, especially when sparkling wine is offered by the glass.

The Garganega grape is used to make Soave, a fresh, lemony white wine that received DOC status in 1968. Another white wine of note is Lugana, which is produced from the Trebbiano di Lugana grape that thrives in the limestone and clay soils along the eastern edges of Lake Garda. Lugana's aromas are floral and fruity.

The best Veneto red wines are based on the Corvina grape. The DOCs of Bardolino and Valpolicella produce excellent blends, where Corvina is dominant. Bardolino DOC reds are a little lighter than Valpolicella wines that are full-bodied and can age very well.

Recommend drinking bottles one to two years after the bottle date.

ITALY:
LOMBARDY

OUTSTANDING	EXCELLENT	VERY GOOD	GOOD	CHALLENGING
2009	2010 2011 2012 2014 2016	2001 2006 2007 2013	2000 2003 2005 2008 2015	2002 2004

Cool continental climate in the foothills of the **ALPS NEAR LAKE COMO.**

Gravel, stony soils are well-drained and rich in minerals.

Pinot Noir (Nero)
Nebbiolo

85%

Chardonnay
Pinot Bianco

15%

Classifications

Lombardy has 5 DOCGs and 21 DOCs. These classifications span red wines, sparkling wines, dessert wines, and white varieties. For the sparkling DOCG Franciacorta, 18 months of aging is required in the bottle prior to release.

Franciacorta DOCG is the best known of the sparkling wines, made with grapes grown on the slopes around Lake Iseo. Chardonnay, Pinot Nero, and Pinot Bianco are permitted.

Valtellina is noted for red wine production, and its wines are made with Nebbiolo. Valtellina has a DOC and a DOCG for its Superiore wines, which must contain 90% Chiavennasca grapes (the local name for Nebbiolo).

Two hours north of Milan, Lombardy has five DOCGs and twenty-one DOCs. They are best known for the sparkling wines of Franciacorta DOCG. Unlike Prosecco, Franciacorta DOCG requires a minimum of eighteen months aging on the lees, similar to non-vintage Champagne. Franciacorta DOCG also requires second fermentation in bottles using the Metodo Classico, very similar to Champagne. Compared to Prosecco, Franciacorta's bubbles are smaller and more complex, and the flavors tend to be nutty and buttery.

Lombardy's other star, Valtellina, is a cherry-scented red made from Nebbiolo. Both DOC and DOCG versions exist. Valtellina takes its name from the alpine valley in northern Lombardy where it grows. Less tannic than Nebbiolo in the Piedmont, Valtellina reds are more delicate and elegant,

yet carry bold flavors. Notes of leather and rose are often found in these well-structured wines that can also age well. Altitudes and steep slopes make the Valtellina winemaking process a labor of love. Because of the topography and the terraces, mechanization is impossible and everything in the vineyards is done by hand.

I also found an amazing dessert wine, Moscato di Scanzo DOCG. It is unique in that it is red (most dessert wines are white) made from the Moscato Nero grape. It also is extremely sweet, with up to ten percent residual sugar and a deep ruby-red color. Unlike some other sweet wines, Moscato di Scanzo is also very well-structured and has a full body while maintaining powerful aromas.

Recommend drinking bottles upon release.

ITALY:
SICILY

OUTSTANDING	EXCELLENT	VERY GOOD	GOOD	CHALLENGING
2005	2006 2007 2012 2014 2015	2003 2004 2008 2010 2011 2016	2000 2002 2009 2013	2001

Mediterranean climate, with a **SUNNY WARM CLIMATE INLAND** with cooler regions at higher elevations.

VOLCANIC SOIL NEAR MT. ETNA.

Nero d'Avola
Nerello Mascalese

50%

Carricante

50%

Classifications

Sicily has 23 DOCs but only a single DOCG. Most wines are produced from co-operatives.

Reds are strong in flavor, but lighter in color. Whites are refined. Sicily's best known sweet wine is Marsala.

In Sicily, the soil is rich, the air fresh, and the rain plentiful. Mount Etna stands on the eastern side of the Island, forever enriching the soil with minerals that are invaluable to grape growing. High in the mountain, you can find more and more modern vineyards, which benefit from the cooler temperatures. Overall, grapes here face few threats of rot or disease and high yields are practically guaranteed. Sicily has just one DOCG—Cerasuolo di Vittoria—and twenty-three DOCs.

The best grape in Sicily is Nero d'Avola, also called "Calabrese" locally. You will find the red Nero d'Avola appearing on many high-end restaurants' wine lists. Within Cerasuolo di Vittoria, Nero d'Avola must age at least eighteen months to carry the "Classico" label. Winemakers may also blend in another Sicilian grape variety called "Frappato" and achieve a minimum of thirteen percent alcohol. The wines of the Cerasuolo di Vittoria DOCG are ruby-red in color, and aromas of red berries and pomegranate are present in the best vintages. Despite the warm weather, there also is a good amount of acidity that balances well with the tannins.

Historically, Sicily may be best known for their Marsala DOC dessert wines. While the quality was poor for a number of years, it has improved over the past decade. Both red and white grapes are used in the production of Marsala, and multiple tiers of strict quality standards exist within the DOC. There are five different types of Marsala depending on the duration of their aging: Fine (one year of cask age); Superiore (minimum two years in cask); Superiore Riserva (minimum four years of cask age); Vergine (aged a minimum of five years) and Vergine Stravecchio (aged a minimum of ten years).

Recommend drinking bottles two to three years after the bottle date.

ITALY:
TRENTINO-ALTO ADIGE

OUTSTANDING	EXCELLENT	VERY GOOD	GOOD	CHALLENGING
2000	2005 2006 2009 2010	2004 2007 2008 2011 2012 2015	2001 2003 2013 2014 2016	2002

Continental climate with **COLD WINTERS** and **WARM SUMMERS.**

Gravel, stony soils are well-drained and rich in minerals.

Lagrein
Schiava

40%

Pinot Grigio
Gewürztraminer
Chardonnay

60%

Classifications

No DOCGs but 9 DOCs in the region. The best wines are from Casteller DOC, Delle Venezie DOC, Südtirol DOC, Etschtaler DOC, and Teroldego Rotaliano DOC.

Whites have high acidity and subtle fruit flavors with mineral character. Generally produced to be consumed within a few years of bottling. Large influence from Germany and Switzerland.

Trentino-Alto Adige (Trentino) is a small valley region in northern Italy defined by its cooperative winegrowers' associations. Geographically, Trentino sits lower in the valley, with altitudes ranging from 120 to 215 meters (393 to 705 feet) above sea level. It has no DOCGs, but nine DOCs that produce ninety percent of all wine in the region. The region is known for high acidity, cool climate white wines made from Chardonnay and Pinot Grigio.

Part of the region was once Austrian, and it maintains that heritage. Cooperatives, many of which use old-world winemaking techniques, are responsible for more than three-quarters of all grapes in the region, whereas large mechanized producers only are responsible for eighteen percent of the region's wine production.

The Südtirol DOC is a very diverse area within the region and produces many typ-ical styles. One of my favorites is the spar-kling wine usually made from a blend of Chardonnay, Pinot Bianco, and Pinot Nero. These wines must age a minimum of twenty months, including fifteen months on the lees. Riserva must age a minimum forty-two months, including thirty-six months on the lees. Like Franciacorta, they also must un-dergo second fermentation in bottles. Süd-tirol DOC sparkling wines are always dry as sweet versions may not be produced.

Schiava is the region's top red grape. Also used for making rosé, Schiava is commonly used to create light wines as the cool tem-peratures are unable to produce full-bodied, complex reds.

Recommend drinking bottles one to two years after the bottle date.

ITALY:
EMILIA-ROMAGNA

OUTSTANDING	EXCELLENT	VERY GOOD	GOOD	CHALLENGING
2001	2000 2004 2006 2008	2009 2011 2013 2014 2016	2002 2005 2007 2010 2012 2015	2003

CONTINENTAL CLIMATE

Limestone soils
situated high above sea level,
more than 1,500 feet
in some areas.

Lambrusco
Sangiovese
Malvasia

50%

Albana di Romagna
Pagadebit di Romagna

50%

Classifications

There are 2 DOCGs and 19 DOCs in the region.
There are three DOC regions for Lambrusco
- Lambrusco di Sorbara, Lambrusco
Grasparossa di Castelvetro, and Lambrusco
Salamino di Santa Croce - as well as a
Lambrusco appellation under the
Reggiano DOC.

Lambrusco is the most noted DOC region with red
sparkling wine, either fizzante or spumante,
but there are no aging requirements. Style can be
either dry or off-dry. Romagna DOC's wines are based
on Sangiovese.

Emilia-Romagna was at one time two separate areas in Italy's northern peninsula. Emilia-Romagna is Italy's second-largest wine-producing region and has two DOCGs, and nineteen DOCs.

Perhaps the most well-known wine in Emilia-Romagna is Lambrusco. Three different Lambrusco DOCs exist within Emilia-Romagna. These can be made as red or rosato (rosé) and either sweet or dry. With crisp and refreshing bubbles, the sparkling wine was once exported and marketed as a sweet and inexpensive wine. Today, Emilia-Romagna producers create several light varieties within the DOC category that range from sweet to dry. Most Lambruscos are made from more than one grape variety and blended together. Unlike some of the other sparkling regions, there are no aging requirements for Lambrusco DOCs.

Colli Bolognesi Pignoletto DOCG produce a sparkling wine from the Grechetto grape in frizzante and spumante styles. Spumante styles are five to six atmospheres of pressure and a full sparkling wine. Frizzante wines are bottled at about half the pressure. They also have a Superiore Classico sparkling wine category that requires at least a year of aging.

Romagna Albana DOCG is best known for a sweet, botrytis-affected wine grapes that are dried on the vine and harvested once they reach a minimum sugar level. Passito and Passito Riserva standards exist that specify the alcohol levels, sugar content, and aging requirements of up to thirteen months.

Emilia-Romagna is also home to other indigenous wines that are rising in recognition, including easy-drinking sparkling wine Ortrugo dei Colli Piacentini DOC and a significant variety of styles from Colli di Scandiano e di Canossa DOC that include a wide variety of local and international red and white grape varieties.

Recommend drinking bottles upon release.

ITALY:
MARCHE

OUTSTANDING	EXCELLENT	VERY GOOD	GOOD	CHALLENGING
2001 2015	2010 2011 2012 2016	2004 2005 2007 2009	2002 2003 2006 2008 2013 2014	2000

MEDITERRANEAN CLIMATE

Calcareous and **LIMESTONE SOIL.**

Sangiovese
Montepulciano

15%

Verdicchio

85%

Classifications

There are 5 DOCGs and 15 DOCs in the region and include both red and white wines. Best wines are from Conero, Castelli di Jesi Verdicchio and Riserva, Offida, Verdicchio di Matelica Riserva, and Vernaccia di Serrapetrona.

Mostly dry un-oaked white wine. Some red wines as well as sparkling whites are made in the region.

Much of the wine produced in Marche is released at the IGT level and not a lot of it is exported outside Italy. There are fifteen DOC and five DOCG appellations, and they are well-worth getting to know.

Diverse terroirs contribute to region's success in producing various contrasting red and white wines. The Verdicchio grape is perhaps one of the region's most renowned and it is credited for Marche's general classification as a white wine region. This grape has sprung from the Marche's ground for more than 600 years. The resulting white wines are green-tinted, dry, and crisp, with notes of lemon.

Long-lived, high-quality reds are produced here as well. For example, Rosso Conero Riserva are made from Montepulciano and Sangiovese grapes. Other red grapes grown in Marche include Pinot Nero and Vernaccia di Serrapetrona, which create a red, spar-

kling DOCG-level wine. Vernaccia can be produced very dry to fully sweet.

Marche's other DOCG-level wine is Offida, which produces both red and white wines, but only the whites are released as DOCG. Made from the indigenous Italian varieties Pecorino and Passerina, Offida represents the exciting potential that lesser-known local grapes. Offida is also well known locally for their varietal Montepulciano which has strong tannins and a bold structure.

The Rosso Piceno DOC has a lower elevation and higher acidity in the wine primarily as a result of the cooling influence of wind currents from the coast. The Sangiovese red wines have a freshness alongside structure and complexity not often seen in the grape.

Recommend drinking bottles three to four years after the bottle date.

SPAIN

When you are looking for solid quality and excellent value, it is hard to go wrong with Spanish wines. It is not surprising that Spain ranks third in global wine production with Tempranillo from Rioja leading the way. Spain's warm weather and reputation for bold red wines has rocketed Spanish wine producers to the top of the global wine market. While Spain's variety in wines may not be as vast as that of France or Italy, you can find outstanding sparkling wines, crisp whites, and light reds alongside bold reds throughout Spain. Distinctively fruitier than mineral-driven French or complex Italian reds, Spain occupies a top spot in the world's wine market and consumers have responded positively.

A challenge for many winegrowers in recent years has been the significant production levels of Spanish wine, lowering prices within the country and the EU. Many larger producers in Spain maintain around-the-clock operations with an industrial production floor and massive bottling capacity. The lower prices for land and labor have also pushed Spain ahead of Italy and France in the export market to satisfy consumer's desire for lower prices.

Spain's approach to winemaking, however, irritates the country's neighbors. In 2016, I was in southwest France a few months after French farmers stopped five Spanish trucks near the border and emptied wine onto the dusty road to protest what they viewed as unfair competition. French wine producers are very concerned about the influx of Spanish wine into the European market and the accompanying competition.

Despite this controversy, Spain's consumer-friendly bottles provide a lot of information such as the producer, vintage, grape variety, and region. If you have a foundational knowledge of the regions and the best vintage years, you should be able to easily choose a bottle that satisfies your preferences.

Spain's quality system has been evolving closer to mirror Italy and France, but is still the most complex from the three in terms of the quality tiers. From lowest to highest, their quality standards include:

- Vino de Mesa (table wine)
- Vino de la Tierra, VT or VdT (wine of the country)
- Vinos de Calidad con Indicación Geográfica (VCIG or VC)
- Denominación de Origen, or DO
- Denominación de Origen Calificada, written DOC or DOCa
- Vino de Pago, or VP

Only fourteen estates hold official VP status, with some awaiting inclusion in the list. These do not apply to regions, but specific estates within the regions. These estates are located mostly within Castilla-La Mancha, Navarra, and Valencia and can be difficult to find in the international market. There also is not much demand or interest from wineries attaining this status.

Only two regions have achieved DOCa status: Priorat and Rioja. Priorat labels its bottles "DOQ"—"Denominació d'Origen Qualificada," which is the translation of the category into Catalan, the local Spanish language. The remainder of the high-quality wines fall into the DO category responsible for about sixty-five percent of all Spanish wine.

The geographic boundaries of each region, grape varietals, yields, percentage of alcohol, and other quality standards are specified and controlled for the wines at each of the different quality standard levels.

Spain historically has been focused on adding designations for aging on the wine labels, unlike France that has embedded aging requirements into the overall standards to use an AOC designation. Spain uses the following terms to designate the aging requirements:

- Gran Reserva red wines may be created from only certain vintages but require at least five years aging, eighteen months of which occur in oak and a minimum of thirty-six months in the bottle.

- Gran Reserva whites and rosés must be aged for at least four years, with at least six months in oak.

- Reserva red wines are aged for at least three years, with at least one year in oak.

- Reserva whites and rosés must be aged for at least two years, with at least six months in oak.

- Crianza red wines are aged for two years, with at least six months in oak.

- Crianza whites and rosés must be aged for at least one year, with at least six months in oak.

Winemakers are not forced to use these labels, however, so their indication of quality is not a sure thing.

SPAIN:
PRIORAT

OUTSTANDING	EXCELLENT	VERY GOOD	GOOD	CHALLENGING
2005 2010	2001 2004 2011 2012	2000 2008 2009 2016	2002 2003 2006 2007 2013 2015	2014

HOT AND DRY Mediterranean climate.

STONY SCHIST SOIL on llicorella with reddish and black slate and small particles quartz.

Garnacha (Grenache)
Cariñena (Carignan)

95%

Garnacha blanca

5%

Priorat is one of only two regions to hold Spain's top-tier DOCa classification. Crianza wines must remain in oak barrels for 6 months and then 18 months in the bottle. Reserva wines must remain in oak barrels for 12 months and then 24 months in the bottle. Gran Reserva wines remain in oak barrels for 24 months and then 36 months in the bottle.

Priorat has moderate acidity, big tannins, and fairly high alcohol, above 14%.

The reds of Priorat are truly amazing and the best in all of Spain. Bold tannins add structure and complexity to this well-balanced wine, resulting in bottles that age extremely well. Deep red cherries and leather flavors pop out of the glass from the best producers, and it is hard not to find a great bottle of Priorat with a lot of consistency within the region.

Located in Catalonia just south of Barcelona, Priorat produces one of the two highest-quality DOCa classifications in Spain. Priorat, however, is miniscule in terms of production. The entire region accounts for roughly 1,600 hectares (3,954 acres), while the other red wine dominant DOCa, Rioja, has more than 60,000 hectares (148,260 acres). Priorat's small size, however, is not a disadvantage.

Red wines dominate Priorat. Garnacha (Grenache) and Cariñena (Carignan) grapes compose the classic Priorat reds, which stem from old vines and unique llicorella soils. These soils are a mix of black slate and quartz that force the vines to go deep to reach water. The resulting wines are dramatically aromatic, with notes of licorice and cherries. A key challenge is to maintain the lower alcohol levels, as the hot weather can produce a lot of sugar that converts to alcohol.

In 2009, Priorat created a new classification within the DOCa region (Vino de Pueblo) for estate-grown wines from twelve villages within Priorat. These include La Morera de Montsant, Poboleda, Porrera, Torroja, Gratallops, Vilella Alta, Vilella Baixa, El Lloar, and Bellmunt, in addition to and three specific areas: Escaladei and the Solanes games (Molar) and Masos (Falset). These wineries must be located in the municipality indicated on the label.

Recommend drinking bottles five to nine or more years after the bottle date.

SPAIN:
RIOJA

OUTSTANDING	EXCELLENT	VERY GOOD	GOOD	CHALLENGING
2010	2001 2004 2005 2008 2009	2007 2011 2014 2015 2016	2000 2003 2006 2013	2002

Continental climate.
Protection from
the Atlantic Ocean
by the Pyrenees and
Cantabrian mountains,
**CREATING A
RAIN SHADOW.**

Tempranillo
Garnacha

Viura

90%

10%

Clay soils, including
**lime rich
calcareous clay.**

Classifications

Rioja wines go beyond Spain's minimum
aging requirements. Rioja is the youngest
and spends less than a year in an oak barrels.
A Crianza is wine aged for at least two
years, at least one of which was in oak.
Reserva is aged for at least three years, of
which at least one year is in oak. Gran
Reserva wines have been aged at least two
years in oak and three years in bottle.

Extended oak time increases the already high tannin levels
and produce an age worthy wine. Deep red colors and vanilla
flavors are some of the most sought flavors in the wines.

Tempranillo reigns over Rioja as one of Spain's top two wine regions. Winemakers in Rioja also blend Tempranillo with other red grapes including Mazuelo, Graciano, and Garnacha. Roughly eighty-five percent of all wine production in Rioja is red wine.

A number of geographic factors make Rioja a great place for wine. The Ebro River is the region's main water source. To the north and west of Rioja, the Cantabrian Mountains create a barrier blocking the Atlantic breeze. The soil is largely limestone, and temperatures are higher than in neighboring regions. The distinctive climate creates three different subregions in terms of terroir: Rioja Alta, Rioja Alavesa, and Rioja Baja.

Rioja Alavesa is a small northern zone that produces mainly vino joven wines for early consumption. Rioja Alta is the southwestern zone, and with a slightly warmer climate produces classic, age-worthy Tempranillos. Rioja Baja, the hottest subregion, contains more alluvial soils and clay—as such, Garnacha dominate Rioja Baja's hot climate. Many Rioja winemakers will also blend grapes from all three of the subregions to produce their wines.

In Rioja, the oak barrels are nearly as important as the grapes themselves. Quality Rioja wines are aged in new French and American oak barrels, contributing complex notes of spice, vanilla, and coconut to the resulting wine.

Rioja goes beyond Spain's DOCa requirements for aging. Red Crianza wines require a total two years of aging prior to release, with a minimum of a year in oak. Red Reserva wines are aged for three years, including one year in oak. Gran Reserva red wines must age for at least two years in oak and another three years in the bottle.

Recommend drinking bottles two to five or more years after the bottle date.

SPAIN:
RÍAS BAIXAS

OUTSTANDING	EXCELLENT	VERY GOOD	GOOD	CHALLENGING
2005	2010 2001 2004 2009 2012 2015	2000 2002 2007 2008 2016	2003 2006 2011 2013	2014

Costal climate with **HIGH RAINFALL** and humidity.

Granite soil covered by mineral-rich alluvial top soils, a combination of clay, silt, sand and granite.

Albariño 99%

Classifications

Rías Baixas follows the Spanish quality standards of Denominación de Origen (DO). Additionally, eight types of wine are permitted in the region: Rías Baixas, Rías Baixas Albariño, Salnés, Condado, Rosal, Barrica (wines aged in oak, can be red or white), Tinto, and Espumoso (sparkling wine).

Stainless steel aging, little to no oak. Pale golden lemon, they are all crisp, elegant and fresh. Bone-dry and aromatic, with natural acidity and mineral overtones. Generally medium bodied with moderate alcohol around 12%.

52

Rías Baixas is not what you think of when you imagine Spanish wine. More aligned with the lush green hills of Ireland and appropriately nicknamed Green Spain, its rainy and cooler climate is at odds with the rest of country, making its white wines all the better for it. With a layer of ocean fog often blocking the views, the climate is cool and wet. The white Albariño grape is prolific throughout the region and many of the best producers make single varietal Albariño. White wine accounts for ninety-nine percent of all wines produced in Rías Baixas.

Situated in northwestern Spain's Galicia region, Rías Baixas has five distinct regions across ninety-seven kilometers (sixty miles) of coastal land, from Galicia's capital city of Santiago de Compostela to the border of Portugal. The subregions are Ribeira do Ulla, Val do Salnés, Soutomaior, Condado do Tea, and O Rosal. The highest concentration of wineries is in Val do Salnés. This region, with its granite and alluvial soils, is also the coolest and wettest subregion.

Albariño wines are crisp and high in acidity, but vary a bit based on the subregion. Val do Salnés wines tend to crisp and aromatic with melon and herbal flavors, while Condado do Tea is earthier and has more minerality. In the region generally, Rías Baixas Albariño wines have elevated acidity and a slightly bitter taste that gives length to the wine. The thicker skins of the grape have salinity, especially in the Val do Salnés, and express apricot and citrus fruit. The Albariño wines of Rías Baixas have a structure that is unique to white wines anywhere in the world.

Recommend drinking bottles upon release.

SPAIN:
PENEDÈS

OUTSTANDING	EXCELLENT	VERY GOOD	GOOD	CHALLENGING
2007 2012	2004 2008 2010 2013 2014 2015	2000 2001 2006 2009 2011	2002 2005 2016	2003

MEDITERRANEAN CLIMATE with a wide variety of micro-climates.

 Garnacha
Tempranillo
Merlot

15%

Sandy, clay-like soil.

 Macabeo
Xarel-lo
Parellada

85%

Classifications

For a wine to qualify for the DO Penedès label, the sample must exceed the minimum quality levels required by the tasting committee and must be sourced from vineyards within the DO Penedès. Cava has its own DO.

The DO Penedès is noted for the best white wines in Spain. 95% of grapes for Cava come from the Catalan region of Penedés.

Penedès has three different zones, all based on altitude: Baix-Penedès, Medio-Penedès, and Alt-Penedès. Penedès is best known for their production of sparkling Cava, produced in the Alta-Penedès.

Cava is a blended wine, like Champagne, but comprised of mostly Parellada, Xarel-lo, and Macabéo (Macabeu) grapes. Cava also has its own DO and is the only DO tied to a style instead of a geography, so it can be made anywhere in Spain. While similar to Champagne, in that Cava is produced with the second fermentation in the bottle, it requires less aging on the lees.

While a little harder to find in the market, Penedès also produces another sparkling wine based on the ancestral method called "Clàssic Penedès." This sparkling wine DO uses grapes that are organically grown, and no additional sugar may be added to the wine. The process of making the sparkling wine is done inside the bottle and then aged for fifteen months in the cellar prior to release. They also have a designation for Reserva, where Clàssic Penedès may age an additional three to fifteen years and then include that number after Reserva. So, a Clàssic Penedès aged for ten years will display "Reserva 10" on the label.

In the lower regions, red grapes thrive, because of the warmer temperatures. Varieties like Garnacha (Garnatxa) and Monastrell are planted in the lower vineyards in Baix-Penedès. These wines produce higher-alcohol red and rosado (rosé) wines. Ull de Llebre (Tempranillo) does well in the Medio-Penedès.

Recommend drinking bottles upon release.

SPAIN:
RIBERA DEL DUERO

OUTSTANDING	EXCELLENT	VERY GOOD	GOOD	CHALLENGING
2010	2001 2005 2009 2011 2015 2016	2004 2012	2000 2002 2003 2006 2013 2014	2007 2008

Continental climate with extremely **HOT SUMMERS** and **COLD WINTERS.**

Mixture of chalk, clay, and limestone.

Tempranillo
100%

Classifications

Cosecha or Joven see no oak. Joven Roble and Joven Barrica are aged for three to six months in oak. Crianza is aged two years with a minimum of one year in oak barrels. Reserva is aged three years, with a minimum of one year in oak. Gran Riserva are only produced in the very best vintages. They are aged a minimum of five years, with a minimum of two years in oak barrels

The high elevation and extreme fluctuation in daytime/nighttime temperatures during the growing season produce well ripened grapes and promote balanced acidity and aromatic complexity.

Northwest of Madrid, the Castilla y León region accounts for a fifth of Spain's land area and some of the most notable wine regions in all of Spain. The Ribera del Duero is the classic Spanish red wine region, with nearly its entire yield consisting of Tempranillo grapes (also called "Tinto del País" or "Tinto Fino"). This highly versatile wine can be consumed very young and express fruity red cherries, and can also be aged significantly in oak and develop leathery tobacco flavors.

The soil in the Ribera del Duero is a complex mix of chalk, clay, and limestone. Annual temperatures range drastically from minus seventeen degrees Celsius (one degree Fahrenheit) to over thirty-seven degrees Celsius (ninety-seven degrees Fahrenheit). Needless to say, scorching hot summers and extreme winters put a strain on the grapes, ultimately restricting the growing season. More than a third of all vines planted in Ribera del Duero are twenty-five years or older, making them stronger, more durable, and exceptionally more weather-resistant than newer vines in other parts of Spain.

A few rosés are also produced within Ribera del Duero. These wines typically have a fruity aroma with notes of wild berries and ripe fruit. The rosés are made from Tempranillos and/or the Albillo grape.

The Regulatory Council of the Ribera del Duero DO places a stamp and a numbered label of authenticity on their wines. There are five labels, which are color-coded according to the type of wine: Gran Reserva, Reserva, Crianza, Rosado, and young red wines.

Recommend drinking bottles two to five or more years after the bottle date.

PORTUGAL

While Portugal does not immediately come to mind when thinking about great wines (except maybe Port), winegrowers in the country offer an amazing combination of high-quality and affordability. Across fourteen eclectic wine regions, robust and expressive reds contrast fresh and crisp whites. Located on the Atlantic coast of western Europe, Portugal benefits from a highly contrasting geography. To the north, the coast is exposed to Atlantic influences and dry and mountainous landscapes. The vineyards of the north-central region, especially Bairrada and Dão, enjoy a more moderate climate than the regions of Lisbon, the Peninsula of Setubal and Tajo which provide the bulk of Portuguese wines.

Portuguese wines are rich in history. Although Portugal created their wine quality system in 1929, Thomas Jefferson and George Washington enjoyed the highly acidic Madeira red wine produced on Portuguese islands 150 years earlier. The Quinta da Foz has been bottling outstanding red wines in the Douro region since 1872 with indigenous grapes that are some of the best in the world.

Choosing a good Portuguese wine is not as tough as other wine regions in Europe as the selection of wines will be a lot smaller compared to France, Italy, or Spain. The export market is very small, and often it will be hard to find Portuguese wines on a menu. When you do find them, the price-points for high-quality wines tends to be comparatively low, as the international demand is not as strong as other regions.

Unlike France and Spain, Portugal has mostly reclassified its wines as either Denominação de Origem Protegida (DOP) or Indicação Geográfica Protegida (IGP) to align with the EU labeling standards. DOP is the superior classification and it includes all Portuguese wines that attained Denominação de Origem Controlada (DOC) status. There are eight DOCs in Portugal: Trás-os-Montes, Lafões, Dão, Bairrada, Beira Interior, Douro Porto, Vinho Verde, and Távora-Varosa.

Like the other EU regions, the quality standards in Portugal are related to strictly-defined geographical boundaries, maximum grape yields, alcohol levels, and recommended and allowed grape varieties. The DOC wines are all officially tasted, tested, and approved to ensure that they meet each region's standards.

After DOC, the next classification is the Indicação Geográfica (IG), or wines with geographical indication. These wines are considered IGP for the purposes of EU protection, or Vinhos Regional (VR) in Portugal. Fourteen of these exist in Portugal. The rules to make a VR wine are much less stringent than those governing DOC wines. Some well-known producers have chosen to use grape varieties that are not permitted for the local DOC classification, but still allows them to receive VR designation. The VR standard provides producers more flexibility, but they still have to meet certain criteria, such as grape variety, geographic restrictions, and minimum alcohol content.

The producer's name is typically prominent on the bottle, as is the region. Any quality standards attained are also typically listed on the front of the label. More information about the producer, grape blends, and style may be located on the back of the label in both English and Portuguese, as well as added information from any importers. For a grape to be listed on the bottle, the wine must contain at least eighty-five percent of that grape.

Portuguese wines may be labeled as "garrafeira," indicating a minimum period of aging before release. Red garrafeira wines must age for a minimum thirty months, including at least twelve months in bottle. White and rosé garrafeira wines must age for a minimum twelve months, with at least six in the bottle before release. The vintage garrafeira Port style has a separate connotation including at least eight years of aging in glass.

Although Portugal is relatively small, it has three distinct climate zones. The northern coast is humid and rainy with a strong influence from the Atlantic Ocean. The southern coast is more Mediterranean with mild winters and warm summers. Inland, away from the Atlantic influence, the climate is dry and hot.

Across this diverse climate hundreds of different grape varieties may be found, with many only known within the local areas that they are grown. The most common red variety is called Castelão, or Periquita. This deep red wine typically has a lot of complexity and spicy, herbal flavors. Red wines comprise about two-thirds of all Portuguese wine. Fernão Pires, or Maria Gomes, is the most common white grape. This highly aromatic grape has light honeysuckle flavors and is great with seafood, or as an aperitif. Portugal's impressive number of grape varieties imparts unique flavors to Portuguese wines, giving them the character and uniqueness that distinguishes them from their European cousins. The geographical and political isolation of the country has allowed Portugal to maintain an extensive collection of more than 300 authorized grape varieties that produce charming and distinctively local wines.

PORTUGAL:
DOURO VALLEY

OUTSTANDING	EXCELLENT	VERY GOOD	GOOD	CHALLENGING
2009 2011	2007 2010 2012 2015	2003 2005 2008 2016	2000 2004 2006 2013 2014	2001 2002

Highly diversified climate. Hot and dry as you move away from the Atlantic. **COOLER, RAINY AND HUMID** toward the coast.

Touriga Nacional
Tinta Roriz
Touriga Franca
Tinta Cão
Tinta Barroca

15%

Donzelinho Branco
Gouveio
Malvasia Fina
Rabigato
Viosinho

85%

The best vineyards have **SCHIST SOIL.**

Classifications

While port is made in the same geography, Duoro DOC are non-fortified wines. Three sub-regions exist: Baixo Corgo, Cima Corgo, and Duoro Superior.

Wines in the region have a wide range in style aged in new oak. The best wines are very dry and powerful red wines.

Named for the Douro River, the Douro Valley in northern Portugal isn't far from Spain's Ribera del Duero. While the region's Spanish neighbor is designated as Tempranillo country, Portugal's Douro Valley is all about Port. Northern Portugal also grows many common international grapes, including Cabernet Sauvignon and Sauvignon Blanc, and many non-Port wines come from the region too. In fact, table wines account for about half of all production in the Douro Valley.

The true stars of this region are the indigenous grapes, which add complexity to Port and table wines alike. A dry, mountainous terroir offers winemakers a variety of soil types. The area's subregions benefit from varying climates within the fluctuating temperature ranges of inland Portugal. Such a terroir allows a diverse list of indigenous grapes to thrive. Among the most popular are Touriga Nacional, Tinta Barroca, Tinto Cão, and Tinta Roriz. Many Douro Valley winemakers plant more than twenty grape varieties in a single vineyard.

Although Ports are often classified as dessert wines, the Portuguese sip them any time of the day or night—often paired with the country's traditional meat-heavy dishes. Port wine is still made using the traditional process throughout the region. This process starts with fermenting wine in non-mechanized lagers. Lagers are fairly shallow open vats that are used to crush the grapes and extract color from the grape skins. The grapes are then crushed for several days. Once the ideal sugar level is reached, brandy is added and then the Port is aged.

While overshadowed by Port, there are a few white wines in Douro as well. A large variety of local grapes—including Moscatel, Gouveio, and Malvasia—are planted at high altitudes to achieve a higher level of acidity in the dry white wines.

Recommend drinking bottles four to five or more years after the bottle date.

PORTUGAL:
VINHO VERDE

OUTSTANDING	EXCELLENT	VERY GOOD	GOOD	CHALLENGING
2013 2014 2016	2008 2009 2010 2011 2012 2015	2006 2007	2000 2001 2002 2003 2005	2004

Cool maritime climate with a **LOT OF RAIN AND HUMIDITY.**

Loureiro
Alvarinho
Trajadura

15%

Vinhão
Borraçal
Amaral

85%

Mostly **GRANITE** soils.

Classifications

Vinho Verde became a classified zone, Denominação de Origem Protegida, or DOP, in 1908. Its geographical boundaries are identical to the Minho region, but the grape-growing and wine-production methods are restricted in order to ensure a recognizable Vinho Verde style.

Low alcohol, high acidy, grassy white wine. Some effervescence in the wines resulting from the injection of carbon dioxide at bottling. Some rosados (rosé) and reds are produced.

Located within the Minho region, Portugal's northernmost wine producing region, Vinho Verde, has cool rainy weather and a very damp growing season. Even with these challenges, Vinho Verde is the largest DOC in Portugal and represents fifteen percent of the nation's total vineyard production. While best known for their fizzy white wines, Vinho Verde creates red and rosato wines as well.

The white grape Loureiro is the region's most heavily planted varietal. The light, floral wines of the region have bright acidity and low alcohol levels. What sets them apart from other white wines is that they are slightly sparkling. This is a result of carbon dioxide injection before bottling. Vinho Verde whites also blend in other grapes to balance the acidity of the Loureiro grape.

Vinho Verde has nine subregions, each producing the same lightly-carbonated wines using a slightly varying blend of grapes. The best of these subregions is Monção e Melgaço, whose unique terroir and hand-picked grapes produce some of the best wine in the region. The climate here is warmer and drier; the maritime influence is partially blocked by hills. These wines are made dry and still.

Red and rosato wines are also produced in Vinho Verde, but in smaller quantities. Produced from grapes like Vinhão, Espadeiro, Borraçal, and Alvarelhão, the red wines are also fizzy. The wines, whether white or red, are best consumed immediately after release. These are not wines to cellar. Vinho Verde wines are released three to six months after harvest and should be consumed within the year.

Recommend drinking bottles six months to two years after the bottle date.

GERMANY

As the northernmost wine region in the world, Germany may qualify as one of the most misunderstood wine regions in the world. Many sommeliers point to Riesling as their favorite grape, and there is nowhere better for Riesling than Germany. The historically cool climate has consistently produced dry Riesling wines with crisp acidity that truly express the fruit and the vineyards where they are grown. Over the last century, however, inexpensive and sweet wines from Germany have flooded the market and given many consumers a distinctly bad impression of German wines. The trend of consumers to seek bold red wines also have caused many buyers to steer clear of the region, even though about forty percent of German wines are reds.

Climate change is benefiting Germany's vineyards as the growing season gets longer and summer temperatures warmer. This trend is triggering even more plantings of red varieties and expansion of vineyards that historically have been in regions too cold to produce quality grapes.

German wine bottles can be somewhat confusing and to understand what you are buying; you must understand the local quality systems. In addition to the producer, vintage, and region, German labels state the quality level of the wine, the grape, the vineyard, and the style. German labels offer a lot of information, but you need to know how to read them.

While Germany did not invent the idea of wine standards, they definitely seem to enjoy creating them. There are many competing systems and rules governing wine quality, as the country has both a traditional and a modern wine quality system. Regions have distinct standards that sometimes run parallel to or conflict with the national guidelines.

Qualitätswein and Prädikatswein represent the two tiers of German wine quality standards. Within Prädikatswein, there are six prädikat levels related to ripeness at harvest of the grape. The prädikat is determined by the level of sugars in the grape at harvest, measured by the Öchsle scale. Generally, the ripeness levels correlate to sweetness, but not always. Kabinett is the initial category, then Spätlese, Auslese, Beerenauslese, Trockenbeerenauslese, and Eiswein.

Kabinett are picked early and produce lighter wines with lower alcohol content and are usually dry. Fruiter and with more body, Spätlese are picked later in the season. Picked in bunches, Auslese grapes are sweeter, as the grapes are very ripe at harvest. Beerenauslese are also very ripe, sweet grapes, but picked individually and not in bunches.

Trockenbeerenauslese wines are not made every year, as the grapes are so ripe they can start transforming into raisins on the vine. They are even affected by botrytis. Trockenbeerenauslese wine is extremely sweet with a low alcohol content because of the significant amount of sugar it contains.

Eiswein grapes are picked well past the traditional harvest, making them very ripe and even frozen. These grapes tend to be quite sweet as the sugars have had abundant time to develop throughout the season. In fact, workers need special protection to pick the grapes given the cold temperatures. Most of Germany's thirteen wine regions are located in the southwestern part of the country. The best vineyards surround the Rhine and Mosel river systems. Historically, these river systems moderate the cool climate and produce better conditions to grow grapes. This location, combined with the blue slate soils that retain heat create ideal locations for Germany's grape varieties. As climate change creates a longer growing season with warmer temperatures, vineyards are slowly migrating northward and the levels of alcohol are increasing as well, as the grapes have more sugar at the time of harvest and fermentation.

Running alongside the Qualitätswein and Prädikatswein system, the Verband Deutscher Prädikatsweingüter, or VDP, is a national German association of producers focused on producing top-quality German wines. Their system focuses on terroir and vineyard site as a measure of quality and is similar to France's system in Burgundy. Their tiers are:

- Grosse Lage: Grand Cru Wines
- Erste Lage: Premier Cru Wines
- Ortswein: Village Wines
- Gutswein: Regional Wines

Two hundred of the best producers are members of the VPD, and you will find the VPD logo on the foil cap of German wines.

The German Wine Institute also created a quality system in the early 1970s based on the sweetness levels of Trocken, Halbtrocken, and Lieblich. While you may see these terms on labels, they do not correspond to quality levels.

GERMANY:
PFALZ

OUTSTANDING	EXCELLENT	VERY GOOD	GOOD	CHALLENGING
2001	2007	2002	2004	2000
2005	2012	2003	2010	2013
2009	2016	2006	2014	
		2008		
		2011		
		2015		

SUNNY AND DRY continental climate, one of the **WARMEST REGIONS IN GERMANY.**

Soil types range from sandstone, limestone, and marl to loess-loam and granite.

Dornfelder
Spätburgunder
(Pinot Noir)

40%

Riesling
Weissburgunder
(Pinot Blanc)
Grauburgunder
(Pinot Gris)

60%

Classifications

Riesling wines from the best, narrowly demarcated sites will bear vineyard names.

Mainly dry white wines are produced in the region, but Pfalz is the largest red wine region in Germany. These age-worthy reds are very popular within Germany. Pfalz white wines have less austere acidity than Mosel. Approachable white wines with a deep bouquet and full body.

To call Pfalz a wine region feels like an understatement. Pfalz, Germany is wine country, where vines outnumber people 600 to one. Pfalz is a narrow space just fourteen kilometers (eight miles) wide and eighty kilometers (fifty miles) long. Pfalz is a natural continuation of France's Alsace, which borders it to on the south.

Geographically, Pfalz is Germany's second largest region, but in terms of production volume, Pfalz often comes out on top. Within the region, 23,000 hectares (57,000 acres) are devoted to grape-growing.

Like many of Germany's other regions, Pfalz produces dry Riesling. The best wineries are from several subregions including Kallstadt, Ungstein, Bad Dürkheim, Wachenheim, Forst, Deidesheim, and Ruppertsberg. Many of the Pfalz wines tend to be pale in color and have some carbon dioxide in the bottle to give it spritz.

Because of the very warm climate, Pfalz also produces a significant amount of red wines as well. Red wines account for forty percent of Pfalz's production. One of the grapes used in red wine production is Dornfelder, which is native to Germany, but Pinot Noir also thrives in the south of Pfalz. Pfalz's grapes grow well in a warm, dry climate, unlike the neighboring regions. This is mostly due to the Haardt Mountains, which create a rain shadow, minimizing precipitation. The Pfälzerwald Forest also acts as a buffer zone, preventing brisk winds from tampering with the vines. In turn, dry summers and mild winters evoke a climate similar to those of Mediterranean vineyards.

Recommend drinking bottles one to three years after the bottle date.

GERMANY:
MOSEL

OUTSTANDING	EXCELLENT	VERY GOOD	GOOD	CHALLENGING
2005	2000	2001	2008	2013
	2004	2002	2010	2014
	2007	2003		
	2009	2006		
	2015	2011		
	2016	2012		

Cold continental climate tempered by the **MOSEL RIVER.**

Riesling
Pinot Blanc
Pinot Gris
Auxerrois

100%

Slate soil retains heat.

Classifications

German wine has two types of classifications. The first is based on quality. Quality is classified into three groupings. Wein does not have a geographic indication. Qualitätswein is from one of thirteen major regions. Prädikatswein is a subset of Qualitätswein based on the ripeness of the grape. Verband deutscher Prädikatsweingüter (VDP) is an association that rates the quality of wine.

Within Prädikatswein, six ripeness levels exist, with the highest quality generally the sweetest. From the lowest to the highest: Kabinett, Spätlese, Auslese, Beerenauslese, Eisweinand, and Trockenbeerenauslese. The first three may be dry or sweet. Low alcohol and stainless steel fermentation are common.

Mosel, the well-known German wine region, is home to the steepest vineyards in the world, growing the best Riesling in the world. Half of the vineyards are rooted at inclines of thirty degrees and more. The steepest slopes sit at a shocking sixty-five degrees.

Across the board, Mosel white wines are light and maintain a low alcohol content. The signature aspect of Mosel Rieslings is intense acidity balanced with some level of sweetness. The floral aromas are subtle, and the color is platinum with an almost greenish hue. The aromas are of medium intensity, and flavors of lemon and honeydew are typically expressed.

The diverse terroirs include clay, sand, and chalky soil, but Mosel may be the best known for their slate. The slate contributes to the wine's intense minerality. Slate is composed of shale, clay, and/or siltstone that is subjected to extreme pressure. In Mosel, winter rains wash away the slate, but workers actually collect it from the rivers and return it to the earth surrounding the vines. Nearly every step in the process is still done by hand, not far off from the region's historic harvest methods that date back to nearly 2,000 years.

Over half of the region's grapes are used in Riesling production, but they have many of the same grapes grown in Alsace including Pinot Blanc, Pinot Gris, and Auxerrois.

As the region snakes around the river, there is a fair amount of variety in the quality of the grapes based on where they sit on the slope and along the river. Some of the most renowned producers like Dr. Loosen, JJ Prüm, and Selbach Oster are gathered near Bernkastle. These wines will be extremely low in alcohol and have a pale color, with some tints of green.

Recommend drinking bottles six months to two years after the bottle date.

GERMANY:
RHEINHESSEN

OUTSTANDING	EXCELLENT	VERY GOOD	GOOD
2007	2001	2008	2000
2015	2002	2009	2004
	2003	2010	2014
	2005	2011	
	2006	2012	
	2013	2016	

Continental climate, circled by protective **HILLS AND FORESTS.**

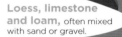

Loess, limestone and loam, often mixed with sand or gravel.

Spätburgunder
(Pinot Noir)
Portugieser

30%

Riesling
Müller-Thurgau
Dornfelder
Silvaner

70%

Classifications

The largest wine region in Germany, there is a wide range of quality. The best vineyards produce a dry Riesling, but many vineyards produce lower quality sweet wine.

The region's reputation was damaged due to the popularization of Liebfraumilch (Beloved Woman's Milk). Originally a high-quality wine from the Liebfrauenstift monastery.

Like other major German wine regions, Rheinhessen's Riesling dominates the region, but the yield is rather small compared to other Germany wine regions. The Müller-Thurgau grape is in decline in the region and thought to be inferior to Riesling. Rheinhessen is home to the world's largest quantities of the Silvaner grape, which creates a dry white wine that locals love to sip in spring. Dornfelder is the most common red grape in the region.

Situated along the Rhine River, from which it gets its name, Rheinhessen has a variety of soils. The village of Westhofen's famous red terroir is the result of sandstone, which has a high concentration of iron. In other parts, you can find chalky soil with small pebbles. The Rhine River in the west further contributes to this ever-fertile land. The rivers, soil, and mild climate allow many crops to flourish in Rheinhessen.

Historically, this region was known for low-quality, inexpensive, sweet wine. Blue Nun and Liebfraumilch flooded the market, and many producers in the region are still producing overly-sweet low-quality wine. Over the last five years, winemakers have been seeking to move beyond this legacy and migrate toward organic winemaking methods, local grapes, and much higher quality standards. The best vineyards are along the western banks of the Rhine.

Rheinhessen is leading the way for a new generation of winemakers that are fusing modern wine-making techniques and capturing traditional methods. The use of local yeasts for fermentation, significantly lower yields, avoiding chemical fertilizers and experimentation with grapes other than Riesling are producing some very interesting new wines from the region. The aromas and flavors tend to be subtler and express an unexpected style.

Recommend drinking bottles one to two years after the bottle date.

GERMANY:
RHEINGAU

OUTSTANDING	EXCELLENT	VERY GOOD	GOOD	CHALLENGING
2012	2000 2001 2004 2005 2006 2009	2002 2003 2008 2010 2015 2016	2007	2014

Cool continental climate with protection from the **TAUNUS MOUNTAINS** and sunlight reflection from the Rhine River.

Slate soil.

Spätburgunder (Pinot Noir)

20%

Riesling

80%

Classifications

Schloss Johannisberg and Kloster Eberbach are two key regions.

Given the slightly warmer climate, wines often have fuller body and are richer. Dry, fruity, and sweet wines are all produced, but the vast majority of Riesling wines are dry.

Riesling grapes have been cultivated here since before medieval times. Rheingau Rieslings tend to have spicy aromas and rich, elegant flavors ranging from mandarin orange to honey and apricot.

The Rhine River, after which Rheingau is also named, is the lifeblood of this small wine region in western Germany. It is along these twenty-five kilometers (fifteen miles) of sloping hills that ninety percent of Rheingau vineyards are rooted. Wineries maximize the river's benefits by planting on the north side of the river so that the vineyards face south. For much of the year, south-facing vines receive more sunlight, and the river reflects even more warmth. As seasons change, the river helps to moderate temperatures, fighting off frost which ultimately lengthens the growing season by a few weeks.

Rheingau wines are light and elegant, with a touch of sweetness and peach flavors. Unlike the Riesling in Mosel, Rheingau will show more fruit as they age. Although stored in oak, the barrels are steamed and neutralized to eliminate the chance of oak flavors coming into the wine. Although the wood flavors are not conveyed, the use of oak provides natural oxygenation and some tannin transfer that adds more body and fullness, especially after several years. Many wines are aged on the lees for several years before bringing them to market.

If you prefer reds, Rheingau's Pinot Noir wines or Spätburgunder wines are smoother in texture and have bold notes of wild berries.

Recommend drinking bottles one to three years after the bottle date.

AUSTRIA

Austria's vineyard area is mostly in east of the country. The four major winemaking regions are Niederösterreich, Wien (Vienna), Burgenland, and Styria (Steiermark). Niederösterreich and Burgenland contain about ninety percent of the country's vineyards.

Austria's culture of small growing plots and quality white wines has existed for only the past thirty years. Before that, the country was known for mass-produced common wines that were even chemically altered to improve the flavor. A major scandal rocked Austria in 1985 and led to over fifty arrests of farmers and producers who laced wine with the sweetening chemical diethylene glycol. This chemical has been shown to cause brain and kidney damage.

As a result of the scandal, Austrian wine laws have been evolving, even as recently as 2016. These standards and a hyper-focus on quality have resulted in some outstanding white wines that are now safe to drink. Depending on the vintage year you purchase, you may see a lot of variety in terms of what is on the labels, as the quality standards have changed a lot over the last decade.

Austrian wine law defines three levels of quality: Wein, Landwein, and Qualitätswein. Qualitätswein, the highest tier, is further classified into the categories of Prädikatswein and Districtus Austriae Controllatus (DAC). Austria mirrored Germany's system for harvest designations.

Ten DACs have been developed so far: Weinviertel, Mittelburgenland, Traisental, Kremstal, Kamptal, Leithaberg, Eisenberg, Neusiedlersee, Wiener Gemischter Satz, and Schilcherland. Each DAC has limited grape varietals, levels of alcohol content, and style characteristics. Other wine regions are currently working to achieve DAC status.

The combination of the Danube river and variety of soils including clay, sand, slate loam, loess all result in a rich intensity to the wines of Austria. White wines overshadow Austria's wine region accounting for over two-thirds of all production. Grüner Veltliner dominates the market and Riesling wines are also excellent. In all, there are thirty-six grape varieties including a red variety called Zweigelt that are found in the classified level wines.

In terms of style, the white wines from Austria are generally drier than wines from Germany from the same grapes and they also may age significantly longer. It is not uncommon to drink white Austrian wines five years or longer after bottling. Drinking the wines younger will still express a freshness and vibrancy, especially as an aperitif before dinner.

Austrian red wines tend to be very light and fresh. Given Austria's cool climate and dry summers, it can be difficult for the Zweigelt to ripen, although the grape is actually the second most planted grape after Grüner Veltliner, in Austria. More vineyards are experimenting with single-varietal Zweigelt, or Zweigelt-dominate red blends in the market. Two other interesting red wines to look for in the market are St. Laurent and Blaufränkisch. St. Laurent reds tend to be medium bodied wines with fresh raspberries aromas and flavors. Blaufränkisch have darker red cherry flavors with much more structure, tannins and complexity.

Although I am not a fan, Austria also produces a sparkling wine called Sekt. It is produced in a diverse number of styles and traditionally served as an aperitif. White and rosé versions exist and most of the glasses I tried were made from Grüner Veltliner, or Grüner Veltliner blends. I found that the bubbles did not express the same charm as still versions of the Grüner Veltliner.

The Austrian Sekt Committee was setup in 2013 to focus on improving the quality of Austria's sparkling wine. One of the initiatives introduced were new quality standards specifically for sparkling wine. The first level "Klassik" establishes that the grapes must have their origins in one of Austria's federal states, as well as stipulating a minimum period of nine months spent on the lees. The second level, "Reserve," must be produced according to the traditional method of fermentation in the bottle. The grapes and base wines must also be grown and vinified in one of Austria's federal states and aged at least eighteen months on the lees. In the top category of bottle-fermented Sekt "Grosse Reserve," the grapes may be harvested only from a single winegrowing community. After a minimum of thirty months bottle-fermentation and maturing on the lees, Sekt in this category may be released to the market no earlier than three years after the harvest. The new quality standards also incorporate additional requirements like hand harvesting, yields and pressing specifications. It will be worth exploring Sekt over the next few years to taste the impact of these changes.

AUSTRIA:
WACHAU

OUTSTANDING	EXCELLENT	VERY GOOD	GOOD	CHALLENGING
2012	2007 2009 2011 2013 2015	2001 2004 2005 2006 2016	2002 2003 2008 2010 2014	2000

Continental climate with the **HOT, DRY SUMMERS** and the harsh winter moderated by the influence of the river Danube.

Zweigelt

10%

Grüner Veltliner
Riesling

90%

Classifications

Wachau, while part of the Niederösterreich region, developed its own classification system of three categories, based on their natural alcohol content by volume. Steinfeder, with 11.5% alcohol, is made with grapes that have just ripened. Federspiel, with a range of 11.5% - 12.5% alcohol, is made with fully ripe grapes. Smaradg, with 12.5% minimum alcohol, is made from very ripe grapes and a rich intensity for a dry white wine.

By law, no wines can show noticeable oak flavors, so neutral oak or stainless steel is used.

If you want to try the best wine in Austria, grab a bottle from Wachau. Small, yet backed by a powerful history, Wachau is the most renowned wine-producing region in Austria. It produces the very best Riesling and Grüner Veltliner wines in Austria. Rieslings from Wachau are consistently rich, whether sweet or dry, while Grüner Veltliner wines contrast with intense aromatics and peppery notes.

Bavarian monks first planted vines on terraced hillsides along the Danube River during the Middle Ages. The best wines from Wachau come from grapes grown in the southern-facing terraces, because they receive the most sun exposure that allows them to fully develop while retaining a high acidity. The river eases the temperatures so that they don't overheat in the sun. Wachau's soil structure is geologically complex and consists of granite, gneiss, and slate, along with alluvial deposits from the Danube River. This contributes to Wachau's incredible mineral white wines.

One of the things that makes Wachau unique from other Austrian regions is its local wine classification system. Winemakers here have developed their own set of standards and classifications. Federspiel wines are the lightest and least ripe with up to 11.5 percent alcohol. Steinfeder wines have 11.5-12.5 percent alcohol, and Smaragd have 12.5 percent alcohol and higher. Smaragd wines are richer and more full-bodied than either Federspiel or Steinfeder and can be quite sweet, on the same level as some of the dessert wines found in both Austria and Germany.

Atypical for white varieties, Wachau's wines are capable of aging for many years, with Riesling in particular being especially age-worthy.

Recommend drinking bottles three to four years after the bottle date.

AUSTRIA:
KAMPTAL

OUTSTANDING	EXCELLENT	VERY GOOD	GOOD	CHALLENGING
2012	2007	2001	2002	2000
	2009	2004	2003	2014
	2011	2006	2005	
	2013	2015	2008	
		2016	2010	

At the intersection of the hot, **PANNONIAN CLIMATE** from the east and cool airstreams flowing down from the Weinviertel.

ROCKY SOIL, gneiss, sandstone loess or gravel.

Zweigelt

10%

Grüner Veltliner
Riesling

90%

Classifications

Kamptal is one of Austria's largest wine growing regions. The town of Langenlois produces the most wine. Kamptal DAC designated wines must have a minimum alcohol content from 12% to 12.5%. Wines bearing the label Kamptal DAC Reserve must have 13% alcohol or more.

Fresh, classical style or powerful reserve wines. Mineral-driven wines with exceptional aging potential. Kamptal DAC wines are dry and made from Grüner Veltliner and Riesling. Kamptal DAC Reserve may be designated if regional flavor elements exist in the wine.

The Kamptal wine region gets its name from the river Kamp that flows directly through it. It also is the home to Langenlois, Austria's largest wine-producing town. Throughout the region, spicy Grüner Veltliner and acidic Riesling dominate the landscape as a classic-styled medium-bodied style and a bold and rich dry Reserve wine.

Grüner Veltliner accounts for sixty percent of all grape production in Kamptal. It presents fresh notes of green apple and grapefruit and a variety of aromas ranging from typical tropical fruits with nutty and smoky impressions.

Riesling, on the other hand, flourishes in Kamptal's northern terraces—particularly in Heiligenstein. Here, clay soils produce rich Rieslings which age exceptionally well. Strong vines produce impressive fruit and finesse, which have a striking mineral impact, especially in the Reserve wines. Depending on soil within the Kamptal region, which can be rock or sandstone, Riesling tastes change from rich and smoky to light and spicy. Common to all Reserve Rieslings is the balanced expression of the fruit with minerality and the clearly recognizable character of the vineyard.

Kamptal's successful white wines thrive in an ideal terroir with sandstone and volcanic soils that are over 270 million years old. The climate of the Kamptal region is an intersection of the hot Pannonian climate from the east and the cool climate of the Waldviertel from the northeast. This convergence causes hot days and cool nights that result in the highly aromatic and distinctive wines with mineral character.

Recommend drinking bottles one to two years after the bottle date.

AUSTRIA:
KREMSTAL

OUTSTANDING	EXCELLENT	VERY GOOD	GOOD	CHALLENGING
2012	2007 2009 2011 2013 2015	2001 2004 2005 2006 2016	2002 2003 2008 2010	2000 2014

The river valley is well protected against **COOL WINDS** from the north while Pannonian climatic influences from the east are significant.

Grüner Veltliner
Riesling

100%

Loess soil over a very compact sub-soil with high **WATER STORAGE CAPACITY** and rock soils are dominant.

Classifications

Kremstal is also part of the Niederösterreich region. Kremstal is divided into three different areas: the original Kremstal Valley, the loess massifs in the east, and the small villages south of the Danube below the Stift Göttweig monastery. The best known vineyards in the region are Pfaffenberg, Kögl, Wachtberg, Sandgrube, Pellingen, Gebling, Spiegel, and Steinbühel.

Fresh, classical style or powerful reserve wines. All stainless steel aging, with no oak.

The vineyards of the Kremstal winegrowing area are located on both sides of the Danube; they extend into the actual Kremstal valley as far as Senftenberg. The historic center of the winegrowing area is the town of Krems, which lies in the far west of the Krems Valley.

Grüner Veltliner and Riesling are the leading varieties of the Krems Valley, representing over seventy percent of the wines. Young Rieslings have a charming fruit flavors and spice that allows them to mature into complex wines after several years. In these wines, the tastes of stone fruit such as peach, apricot, and exotic tropical fruits dominate the glass. The wines also have mineral notes of slate. Older bottles will express more rose-like aromas. The best Grüner Veltliner wines from Kremstal will deliver zesty lemon flavors with distinct minerality. A substantial structure with fine fruit extracts dominates the long finish.

Cool, humid northern breezes collide with warm, dry eastern winds, moderating the climate and allowing the grapes to develop.

The wines may be labeled either Classic or Reserve, with a corresponding minimum alcohol content of either twelve or thirteen percent. Reserve wines may have elements of botrytis and wood and generally will have a richer, fuller-bodied wine, but Classic-labeled wines must be spicy and have no wood or botrytis flavors.

When comparing wines from the Kremstal to other Austrian wine regions, generally you will find Kremstal wines to have a lighter style and much more delicate fruit aromas and flavors. Even wine experts may have trouble distinguishing Kremstal wines from Kamptal wines, as they have a very similar style. The delicate flavors are enhanced by many of the producers that have also shifted to biodynamic and organic wine production in Kremstal. You will find some red wines in the regions, but I recommend sticking to the whites.

Recommend drinking bottles one to three years after the bottle date.

UNITED STATES

With a geographic area as large as all of Europe, the United States is the fourth largest producer of wine globally. The United States has half a dozen significant wine regions and several subregions. California, the largest producer of wine, has four major growing regions: North Coast, Central Coast, South Coast, and the Sierra Foothills. In turn, each of these regions includes a number of smaller American Viticultural Areas (AVAs)—for example, the Napa Valley AVA and Sonoma Valley AVA are both located within the North Coast AVA.

In the United States, though, one common trait is that terroir takes a back seat to the grapes. The Bureau of Alcohol, Tobacco, and Firearms (ATF) implemented a system of appellations based on distinctive geography and climate features in 1980, but even after almost thirty years, consumers are unfamiliar with most of these designations. AVAs are mostly unknown to consumers, even in the region. Instead, wine producers promote the grapes and the varieties used on their labels.

Since the United States has become the leading consumer of wine in the world, wine producers in other countries have been altering their labels and production to meet the preferences of these consumers. Some of these alterations focus on adding grape names to the labels and creating lower price point vintages for export to the United States market.

The major difference between AVAs and the European quality systems is that the standards to label a wine within the AVAs do not specify grapes, styles, or parameters on how wines from that AVA should be produced. The only requirement is that a significant percentage of the grapes used in that wine come from the geography within the defined AVA. For a winemaker, there is a lot more freedom to produce a wine in the United States without the perception that it does not have a prescribed quality label and as a result at a lower price point.

Within the United States, California dominates the market. In fact, all of the other states combined have fewer wineries than all of California, as the state produces almost ninety percent of all wine in the United States.

The sophistication of the United States wine market is even more profound, considering that alcohol was completely banned in the United States from 1920 to 1933, devastating the commercial wine market. For the next thirty years, the wine industry struggled to recover, and it was not until the late 1960s that higher-quality wine was produced. Massive investments from American wine pioneers like Robert Mondavi, Joe Heitz, and Louis Martini in state-of-the art production facilities and highly-scientific techniques have propelled the United States wine market over the past fifty years.

Beyond California, the wine regions migrate north into Washington State and Oregon on the West Coast and then cross the country where New York, Virginia, and other wine regions flourish on the East Coast.

Across these regions and tens of thousands of commercial wineries, over 300 grape varieties are grown. Cabernet Sauvignon, Pinot Noir, Viognier, Riesling, Zinfandel, Pinot Gris, Syrah, and Sauvignon Blanc are all common.

Stylistically, the warmer regions in California tend to express a lot of fruit and have higher alcohol levels. On the west coast, as you travel north, the alcohol levels drop and slightly less fruit is conveyed. Gone are the intense buttery California Chardonnays from past decades; replaced with more nuanced oak aging, subtle fruit and balance. Red, white, rosé, sparkling, sweet, dry; whatever style you are seeking, you will find quality examples in the United States.

Across the world, when I spoke with winemakers, all expressed respect and some envy about wine regions in the United States. It was not because of the consistent quality or unique grape varietals, but the freedom to create wines with an open palate of grapes and process. Unlike the old-world regions, the United States' spirt of innovation and creativity extends deeply into the wine market and that flexibility is not often available to European winemakers.

UNITED STATES:
NORTH COAST

OUTSTANDING	EXCELLENT	VERY GOOD	GOOD	CHALLENGING
2013	2002 2005 2007 2008 2009 2012 2014	2001 2003 2004 2006 2010 2016	2000 2015	2011

COOL MARITIME climate on the coast and warm to hot inland.

OUTSTANDING	EXCELLENT	VERY GOOD	GOOD	CHALLENGING
2014	2002 2003 2004 2008 2012 2013	2005 2006 2007 2009 2010 2015	2000 2011 2016	2001

Mountain ranges either block or funnel cool air from the **Pacific Ocean inland** depending on the orientation.

Large range of soil types from volcanic soils, red and white clay as well as sandstone.

 Merlot, Cabernet Sauvignon Zinfandel, Pinot Noir

55%

 Sauvignon Blanc Chardonnay

45%

Classifications

American Viticultural Areas (AVAs) that refers to the specific geographic locations. There are four major wine subregions:

1. Napa
2. Sonoma
3. Mendocino
4. Lake

With the warmer weather, red wines tend to be higher in alcohol compared to old world wines. A wide range of styles including single grape varieties, blends, and sparkling wine. The quality of the grapes and the production process are emphasized over the concept of terroir.

In California's North Coast, during the eighteenth century, Spanish missionaries planted vineyards everywhere they went. The original vines came from Mexico and eventually became known as the "Mission Grape." Missionaries used wine for religious sacraments and everyday drinking. The Gold Rush in the mid-nineteenth century increased the population and the demand for wine. The first commercial wineries were established in the Sonoma Valley in 1857 and the Napa Valley in 1859.

The North Coast includes the most iconic California wines. Napa Valley, Sonoma County, Mendocino County, Lake County, and Marin and Solano Counties are all in the North Coast. Napa and Sonoma are the best-known. Within the Napa Valley AVA, there are fourteen other AVAs and thirteen within the Sonoma County AVA. Each subregion has distinct microclimates and soil formed by a diverse landscape of hills, sun exposures, and elevations. About 400 wineries are in Napa

and 260 in Sonoma, although geographically Sonoma is about double the size of Napa.

Within the North Coast, the Mediterranean-like climate and a long, constant growing season produces grapes that can be quite ripe. These wines, as a result, typically have a higher alcohol content and fruit-forward flavor. Hot inland temperatures and cool air from the Pacific Ocean produce warm days and cool nights, creating an ideal growing climate for grapes of all kinds.

Cabernet Sauvignon, Merlot, Chardonnay, Zinfandel, Sauvignon Blanc, Syrah, and Pinot Noir are the most prominent wine grapes. Riesling, Sangiovese, Pinot Grigio, Muscat, and Malbec are also among the extensive assortment of grapes that North Coast winemakers use to produce both traditional and contemporary wines.

Recommend drinking bottles three to five or more years after the bottle date.

UNITED STATES:
WILLAMETTE VALLEY

OUTSTANDING	EXCELLENT	VERY GOOD	GOOD	CHALLENGING
2012 2006 2016	2004 2008 2013 2014 2015	2001 2005 2009	2000 2010 2011	2002 2003 2007

Cool maritime climate, with a **RAIN SHADOW** protecting the region from Pacific Ocean storms.

Pinot Noir
Cabernet Sauvignon

70%

Chardonnay
Pinot Gris
Riesling

30%

Soil is a mix of alluvian, **VOLCANIC, AND CLAY.**

Classifications

Oregon labels within the Wilmette American Viticultural Area (AVA) must contain 100% of grapes from Oregon. 95% of the grapes must be from that appellation. The Willamette Valley has several sub-AVAs.

Pinot Noir dominates the region and is typically aged in oak barrels. The wine style is less fruity compared to California wines and exhibits stronger earthier flavors. While red wine dominates the region, Chardonnay and Pinot Gris are excellent in the region as well.

Oregon can be considered the wine world's up-and-comer, and this Pacific Northwest state shows a promising future. Tucked between the Coast Range and Cascade Mountains in western Oregon, the Willamette Valley is a region that stretches 195 kilometers (120 miles) south of Portland.

Viticulture took root in Oregon when students from the University of California-Davis began to experiment with Pinot Noir in the 1960s. A Pinot Noir wine from the Willamette Valley is typically lighter than a Burgundy wine, but has more minerality than a Californian wine. An Oregon Pinot Noir placed in the top three wines at the Gault-Millau French Wine Olympiads in 1979, even outranking several wines from Burgundy. Ever since, Oregon wine country has been practically synonymous with Pinot Noir.

Today, Pinot Noir accounts for sixty percent of statewide wine production. The subtle, earthy flavors and aromas are consistent from vintage to vintage, with notes of black cherries, berries, and mushrooms. Six smaller AVAs sit within Willamette Valley: Dundee Hills, Eola-Amity Hills, Ribbon Ridge, McMinnville, Yamhill-Carlton District, and Chehalem Mountains. While the AVAs are small geographic areas similar to Burgundy, there are a number of climatic and soil differences that allow each area to express different flavors in the wines.

Willamette Valley's Pinot Noir has strong roasted spices flavors in addition to black raspberries and cocoa. I find the classic varieties to be elegantly textured and seamlessly integrated, with silky and polished tannins. There are also some excellent white wines from Willamette Valley, but they are typically overshadowed by Pinot Noir. A number of white wines including Pinot Gris, Chardonnay, and Riesling are excellent.

Recommend drinking bottles two to four years after the bottle date.

UNITED STATES:
COLUMBIA VALLEY

OUTSTANDING

2005
2012

EXCELLENT

2001
2002
2014
2006
2009
2010

VERY GOOD

2007
2013
2015
2016

GOOD

2000
2003
2008
2011

The Cascade Mountains protect the Columbia Valley and produce a rain shadow from the cool and rainy weather from the Pacific Ocean. The Columbia Valley has a continental climate as a result with **HOT AND DRY** summers.

Syrah
Cabernet Sauvignon
Merlot

60%

Riesling
Chardonnay

40%

GRANITE AND SAND.

Classifications

The Columbia Valley American Viticultural Areas (AVA) includes 99% of the total vineyard area planted in the state of Washington. With the exception of Puget Sound and Columbia Gorge, all other growing regions in Washington are sub-appellations of the Columbia Valley.

The unique climates of the area allow the Columbia Valley to produce wines that are very fruit-forward, similar to California wines, but with additional structure and earthiness of European regions.

As the second largest wine-producing state in the country, Washington State is home to the Columbia Valley AVA. This dry and sunny region of the Pacific Northwest produces nearly ninety-nine percent of the state's wines and encompasses more than 20,000 hectares / 50,000 acres of vineyards. Think of the Colombia Valley as a nesting doll. Within the Columbia Valley are twelve sub-appellations including Yakima Valley, Walla Walla Valley, and Horse Heaven Hills. Inside the Yakima Valley lie three AVAs: Snipes Mountain, Rattlesnake Hills, and Red Mountain. Here, some of the very best Cabernet Sauvignons in the region are produced.

Shaped by the Ice Age-era Missoula Floods over 20,000 years ago, the unique terroir of eastern Washington is enriched by Lake Missoula. A desert-like climate, high winds, cold nights, and nearly 300 days of sunlight annually create a unique climate for the grapes. The famous soil is a combination of the Missoula Floods' sediments topped with a layer of wind-blown silt known as "loess." The result is a sandy soil known as the "Warden silt loam." This soil allows grapes' roots to reach through the wind-deposited soils, deep into the microscopic silt carried over from the historic floods. Meanwhile, natural fresh water from the Cascade Mountains' snowmelt and the Columbia River compensate for the region's limited rainfall, which amounts to about fifteen centimeters (six inches) annually. These distinctive environmental factors produce aromatic, fruit-forward reds and fresh whites.

Irrigation is also critical for Washington vineyards. This allows growers to cultivate wines in an otherwise arid region. As a result, Riesling and Chardonnay have flourished in Washington since the 1970s, although about sixty percent of all Washington wines are reds.

Recommend drinking bottles three to four years after the bottle date.

UNITED STATES:
FINGER LAKES

OUTSTANDING	EXCELLENT	VERY GOOD	GOOD	CHALLENGING
2004	2001 2007 2010 2015	2012 2013 2014	2000 2002 2003 2006 2008 2016	2005 2009 2011

BITTERLY COLD WINTERS
and short growing season. Highly variable climate, especially over the last decade. The large lakes moderate the climate in the winter to allow grapes to grow in the region.

Complex soil
environment with a mixture of limestone, shale, gravel, and silt.

Pinot Noir
Cabernet Franc

10%

Riesling
Gewürztraminer
Chardonnay

90%

Classifications

The Finger Lakes region centers on the four main lakes: Canandaigua, Keuka, Seneca, and Cayuga. The latter two having their own American Viticultural Areas (AVA) status.

Best known for clean, intense Rieslings aged in stainless steel. Often compared to German wine regions based on the short growing season and climate. Many examples of dry Rieslings of outstanding quality exist across over 100 different wineries.

At first glance, New York State seems an un-likely candidate for grape-growing. After all, this northeastern state faces much harsher winters than West Coast vineyards. Nev-ertheless, New York remains the country's third largest wine-producing state (after California and Washington) and is home to the Finger Lakes region.

So, how do the vines survive the early frosts? In the Finger Lakes, large bodies of water regulate temperature by insulating the vine-yards during the winter and bringing down temperatures in the summer. As a result, vines can continue to grow during the cold season without the threat of frostbite.

The vineyards along these lakes are cred-ited with world-class Rieslings, one of the only internationally-prized wines from the East Coast. Rieslings from the Finger Lakes can be both sweet and dry. Typically, they are aromatic. The Rieslings from the Finger Lakes have a creamy mouthfeel and long finish with pears and tangerine, and some citrus flavors. The wines balance tart acidity, subtle earthiness, and stone fruit.

While Pinot Noir is also produced within the Finger Lakes, I find that the region is just a bit too cold to produce quality Pinot Noir. As climate change continues to make this region warmer, similar to Germany, it may be able to produce increasingly superior reds in the coming years.

Many of the winemakers handpick the grapes and use natural yeast from the region. The fermentations can be long using this approach, especially with the cooler weather, but results in a more natural and biodynamic wine.

Recommend drinking bottles six months to two years after the bottle date.

UNITED STATES:
MIDDLEBURG

OUTSTANDING	EXCELLENT	VERY GOOD	GOOD	CHALLENGING
2001 2014 2015	2006 2007 2010 2012 2016	2004 2005 2009 2013	2002 2003 2011	2000 2008

Highly diverse climate with the Blue Ridge and Appalachian Mountains to the west and the Chesapeake Bay and Atlantic Ocean to the east. **SIGNIFICANT RAIN, HUMIDITY,** and fairly short growing season produce variable weather from year to year.

Cabernet Franc
Merlot
Cabernet Sauvignon
Petit Verdot

60%

Chardonnay
Viognier

40%

CLAY AND LIMESTONE
are found throughout the state but overall the soil is variable depending on the specific area.

Classifications

The Middleburg AVA is in the northern Piedmont area and is a one drive hour west of Washington D.C. The region is bounded by the Potomac River to the north and the Blue Ridge Mountains to the west. The wineries tend to be clustered north of the town of Purcellville and southwest of the town of Middleburg.

Virginia produces many different styles of both red and white wines. Red single varietals, and Merlot-based Bordeaux blends are common. Crisp, single varietals and white blends are also produced in the region.

Winemaking in the United States was born in Virginia, but it did not last. Although Virginia winemaking began in the seventeenth century, the industry never flourished and ultimately ended during Prohibition. Generally, the Virginia market has exploded in the last thirty-five years. Today, the mid-Atlantic commonwealth has accumulated more than one hundred wineries, ranking it fifth in the country's list of largest producers.

Not unlike the Piedmont hills in Italy, sloped vines facing southwest are common. Microclimates are typical based upon small changes in air movement and terrain throughout the AVA, especially in the summer when the humidity can be quite high. The fact that the soil does not retain a lot of water is critical in the best sites.

The climate in the Middleburg AVA is a mixed bag. Vineyards benefit from a temperate climate where the nearby Atlantic coastline and influence from the Chesapeake Bay helps moderate the average temperatures from season to season. Some of the greatest challenges, however, can include hurricanes, very humid summers, diseases and pests on the vines throughout the growing season.

In terms of grapes, both red and white varietals are common. Some of the best white wines are made with Viognier, but you will also find a lot of Chardonnay. For the red varietals, Cabernet Sauvignon and Cabernet Franc are the best. You will also find French-American hybrids as well as the native American grapes, Norton in the region.

In terms of style, the Virginia reds remind me of Right Bank Bordeaux wines. They have a graceful opulence of body and duration of finish. The layered red fruit and leather and coffee flavors are well-balanced and complex. The rich texture and ruby color are outstanding, and the wines have strong tannins, but not enough to disrupt early drinking.

Recommend drinking bottles one to four or more years after the bottle date.

ARGENTINA

Argentina has been hit hard by climate change, seeing some of the most challenging growing seasons in recent years. Overly hot and dry weather has made the processes of growing their quality Malbec red wines more challenging. The Zonda—a strong, dusty, hot wind that blows down from the mountains in the late spring and early summer—has become more intense in recent years. With other problems like overproduction leading to lower quality, great wine from Argentina can be difficult to spot.

The winemaking regions in Argentina are divided among five growing regions. In the north, Salta and Catamarca are in the northwest region around the Calchaquí Valley. The region of La Rioja is characterized by having a dry climate, with warm days and cool nights. The San Juan region is 630 meters (2,067 feet) above sea level. The central provinces of Cuyo includes Mendoza, and finally the South Argentine region including the Patagonian vineyards on the banks of the Limay, Neuquén, Negro, and Colorado rivers. Almost three-quarters of the country's wine production, though, occurs in Mendoza.

Argentina utilizes three levels of quality designations:

- Indicación de Procedencia, or IP – table wines which contain at least eighty percent of grapes from the region

- Indicación Geográfica, or IG – higher-quality wines grown, produced, and bottled in a specific area

- Denomination of Origin (DOC) – which are Argentina's top-quality wines, but are very few in number and can be difficult to find in the market.

Winemakers label both red and white wines as "Reserva" or "Gran Reserva." "Reserva" implies a minimum six months of aging for white wines and one year for reds. "Gran Reserva" indicates at least one year of aging for whites and two years for reds.

The key geographic trait that makes wines from Argentina amazing is the altitude. Historically, the snowcapped Andes brought abundant water to the lower lying vineyards, sometimes causing the vineyards to flood. As new sites have developed, and climate change brings less water from the Andes, the country is struggling to find new sources for water in this arid region, with little rainfall. Hailstorms are quite common, as are cold winters and early spring frosts. Still, the consistently sunny weather, low humidity and daily temperature shifts make Argentina an ideal location for grape growing.

Although the soils in this large country are diverse, most of the vineyards sit on sand. Under the sand lies clay, limestone or gravel; each subsoil providing different characteristics to the grapes.

The history of wine in Argentina goes back to the early colonial era. In 1556, Father Juan Cedrón brought some vine stakes from Chile and established the first winery in Argentina. These cuttings were intended to be used for communion wine, not for general consumption. Three hundred years later, in 1852, Argentine President Domingo Faustino Sarmiento hired a French agronomist, Michel Aimé Pouget, to come to Mendoza and plant a vineyard. Aimé Pouget introduced the French varieties Cabernet Sauvignon, Merlot, Pinot Noir and Malbec. The dry climate, runoff from the mountains and high altitude helped produce excellent crops. Around 1880, Tiburcio Benegas planted a vineyard and built a large-scale winery: "El Trapiche" which today is the largest producer of wine in Argentina. With the arrival of the railroad to the Province of Mendoza in 1885 the winery was able to supply Buenos Aires with locally produced wines. From those original French varieties planted, Malbec flourished.

Immigrants from Spain and Italy developed the wine culture in Argentina in the early 1900s. The wine industry is still very young, only developing high quality wines over the past thirty years. Many new winemakers are still working to find their footing and define their signature profile. While over 100 grape varieties are planted in Argentina, almost seventy percent of the production is red. Malbec is the dominant red grape with a fruit-forward, aggressive and chewy character. The Malbec wines from Argentina tend to have higher alcohol levels, almost black in color and full body. A current trend, however, is to limit the water supply to the grapes or harvest earlier to reduce the ripeness and sugar content. This produces a more subtle and refined Malbec, not recently found in Argentina. Torrentés is growing in popularity from the white varieties, with fresh fruit and intense flowery aromas. Chardonnay is also common, with a rich and powerful style unlike what you will find in California or Burgundy.

ARGENTINA:
MENDOZA

OUTSTANDING	EXCELLENT	VERY GOOD	GOOD	CHALLENGING
2002 2006	2003 2009 2010	2005 2011 2013	2000 2004 2007 2008 2012	2001 2014 2015 2016

CONTINENTAL CLIMATE with an arid and dry climate. Very strong Zonda wind prevents mildew and diseases on the vines.

ALLUVIAL SOIL with rocky subsoil.

Malbec
Syrah
Tempranillo
Cabernet Sauvignon

60%

Sauvignon Blanc
Chardonnay

40%

Classifications

The best red wines are found in Mendoza's high altitude wine regions of Lujan de Cuyo and the Uco Valley. These areas are located at the foothills of the Andes mountains.

Many of Malbec's wines spend 6 months aging in oak. Some age for 10-12 months or 18-20 months, with a significant increase in cost for the additional aging.

Situated along the eastern foothills of the Andes, Mendoza is easily Argentina's most important wine region—the one that puts the country on the world wine map. It is largely dedicated to red wine production, with Malbec leading the way as its most popular variety.

The Andes Mountains cause a rain shadow effect, which results in a relatively low annual rainfall. With the hot and dry climate, irrigation is necessary for many of Mendoza's vineyards. The region's mountainous terrain is a crucial aspect of its terroir. At such high elevations, the Malbec grapes benefit from a long growing season and cooler night temperatures, allowing them to ripen to perfection while maintaining acidity. These factors ultimately lead to the development of well-balanced, high-quality wines.

The Malbecs from Mendoza are distinguished for a number of factors. The wine has an intensely dark color. The aromas are range from cherries, strawberries, and plums, to raisins and black pepper. In the mouth, Malbec is warm, soft, and sweet, with tannins that are not aggressive, but sweet and silky. When it is aged in wood, it acquires shades of coffee, vanilla, and chocolate.

Mendoza is broadly divided into Northern, Central (Upper), Southern, Eastern sectors, and the Uco Valley. Luján de Cuyo and the Uco Valley are the two most important and sought-after subregions of Mendoza's high-altitude wines. Luján de Cuyo has one of Argentina's two DOCs, authorized only for Malbec wines.

Mendoza also produces Cabernet Sauvignon, Syrah, Sauvignon Blanc, and Chardonnay, but most vineyards are dedicated to Malbec. As more winemakers branch out from Malbec production and experiment with other grape varieties, consumers can expect to see an influx of new Mendoza wines come to market in the coming years.

Recommend drinking bottles three to four years after the bottle date.

ARGENTINA:
SALTA

OUTSTANDING	EXCELLENT	VERY GOOD	GOOD	CHALLENGING
2009	2006 2010 2013	2003 2005 2011 2012	2000 2002 2004 2007 2008 2014	2001 2015 2016

TEMPERATE CLIMATE
with diurnal shifts. Very dry, averaging only eight inches of rain per year. Vine training and drip irrigation is needed. Salta may have the highest elevated vineyards in the world.

Malbec
Syrah
Tannat

60%

Torrontés

40%

SAND AND RUGGED
above a clay base.

Classifications

The most outstanding wine subregion is Cafayate, in the Calchaquíes Valleys. This area concentrates 70% of the vineyards in Salta.

While only responsible for 1% of Argentina's wine, Salta is best known for Torrontés, one of the most floral wines in the world and high-tannin red Malbec wines.

Salta may be small, but it is certainly unforgettable. Argentina's northernmost region produces only about one percent of the country's wines, yet it is home to some of the most extreme winemaking conditions in the world, with vineyards 3,000 meters (9,843 feet) above sea level and closest to the equator.

In the colorful Andes of Salta, this terrain may prove tough for breathing, but it is excellent for winemaking. The Andes Mountains provide a rain shadow that blocks rainfall and offers natural irrigation from melting snow. The soil is sandy and dry, not unlike that of Mendoza.

The best wine is Salta is Torrontés, and the best place to find it is within Cafayate. This is an up-and-coming region within Salta and is increasingly appearing on bottles of Torrontés. Torrontés wines are the most aromatic in the world, with a perfume of honeysuckle and lavender. The high growing altitudes give them a light and crisp flavor.

Salta is also home to rich Malbec, Syrah, and Tannat wines. Tannat, which is less widely known, is a dark red with high acidity and high tannins. Malbec, Tannat, Cabernet Sauvignon, and Syrah receive intense sunlight and their skins thicken to safeguard against the sun. The grapes take longer to mature, and tannins are then concentrated, producing amazing age-worthy red wines.

Another significant subregion in Salta is the Calchaquí Valley. Here, temperatures shift dramatically from day to night. A brutal thirty-seven degrees Celsius (ninety-nine degrees Fahrenheit) at noon and can drop to merely ten degrees Celsius (fifty degrees Fahrenheit) at night. In the winter, temperatures are cold.

Recommend drinking bottles upon release.

CHILE

About 4,800 kilometers (2,982 miles) long and only 160 kilometers (100 miles) wide, Chile is wedged between the Pacific Ocean and the Andes Mountains. Chile's climate varies incredibly from the northern to southern latitudes. In the north are dry and desert-like conditions. In the middle of the country, the proximity to the Andes Mountains cools nighttime temperatures; and along the southern coast, the cold, maritime Humboldt Current chills the vines. These combinations of factors make Chile an ideal location for viticulture.

Winemaking is Chile is not a recent phenomenon; in fact, it is over 500 years old. The last twenty years, however, have brought radical change to the wine production pushing Chilean wines to the top of the quality spectrum. Even as late as the 1990s the primary grape planted was País, a native red variety. Carmenère, imported from Bordeaux and confused as Merlot until the mid 1990s, was also widely grown. Most wines were single varietals, blended with grapes from many different parts of the country. The concept of terroir and an expression of place in the wine did not exist.

Then, a significant shift occurred and changed the face of Chilean winemaking. More internationally known varieties like Cabernet Sauvignon, Chardonnay, Sauvignon Blanc and Merlot were planted and Chilean wine was rebranded. At the same time, a focus on producing wine from the distinct wine regions occurred alongside the desire to express particular aspects of the climate and soil in the wine. Many new wineries were established in areas like Casablanca and the San Antonio Valley that brought Sauvignon Blanc, Pinot Noir and Chardonnay to market.

Today, some winemakers today are returning to experiment with País and Carmenère either as single varietals or blends for their wine. These vintners are trying to retain Chilean "roots" while expressing the regions through those traditional grapes. While most of the wine production from Chile are red varieties, there are some outstanding white wines as well.

In Chile, six regional Denominations of Origin (DOs) exist. From north to south, these are Atacama, Coquimbo, Aconcagua, the Valle Central (Central Valley), Sur (the Southern Regions), and the Austral Region. Unlike the European classification systems, Chile does not restrict grape varieties or production practices. Instead, they focus on geography and percentage of grape consistency. That means that on the labels, the grape used is listed most prominently. Chilean wine law requires that the stated grape, vintage, and geographical area, or DO, compose seventy-five percent of what is in the bottle.

Other terms like "Reserva," "Reserva Especial," "Reserva Privada," and "Gran Reserva" refer to the level of alcohol and time aging, but unlike other wine regions, no true quality standards exist for these terms. Instead, it is important to know the specific producers and understand the wide variety of soils that exist within the country to select outstanding wines. In the west, slate, granite and schist soils dominate while clay, silt and sand are located in the central regions. Each soil type will have a different impact on the wines.

Chile is also famous in the wine world for being free of phylloxera. Phylloxera is a tiny insect that lives in and eats the roots of grapevines. Between the late 1860s and 1890s, the pest almost completely wiped out Europe's vineyards. All of the winemakers needed to replant one hundred percent of their vineyards with new vines grafted to American rootstock, which is immune to phylloxera. Chile was not subject to phylloxera given their geographic isolation in the world, strict import controls, soil composition and irrigation techniques.

In terms of style, Chile is best known for their red wines. The most important grape is Cabernet Sauvignon comprising over half of all vineyard plantings. These Cabernet Sauvignon wines gained international attention over the years, the most famous being Don Melchor, from Viña Concha y Toro, which regularly achieves first place rankings in international competitions. Cabernet Sauvignon wines from Chile are typically fruity and concentrated with a high level of tannins. The aroma of these wines is marked by blackcurrant, and some herbal tones. Merlot and Carménère are also planted but in numbers far less than Cabernet Sauvignon. I find Carménère, however, to be one of the best grapes in Chile. Its characteristics are a deep red color with a berry aroma; fruity and intense. The concentration of tannins is not as high as in the Cabernet Sauvignon, which positions Carménère as a lighter wine. The traditional grape of Chile is País, which was brought by the Spanish. While not significantly represented in winemaking, some producers are experimenting with País and trying to bring this traditional grape back into the mainstream.

Sauvignon Blanc and Chardonnay represent the outstanding white wine grapes in Chile. These wines are fresh, fruity, and stand out for their extraordinary body. Sauvignon Blanc is characterized by having subtle aromas of hay and gooseberry, in addition to an intense acidity. Varieties grown in warm areas are ideal for barrel aging. In Chile, the Casablanca Valley offers near perfect conditions for Chardonnay. Among its qualities, its refined melon aromas stand out.

CHILE:
CENTRAL VALLEY

OUTSTANDING	EXCELLENT	VERY GOOD	GOOD	CHALLENGING
2007	2003 2005	2000 2001 2004 2012 2013	2002 2006 2008 2009 2010 2011	2014 2015 2016

DRY AND HOT with cool ocean breezes.

The soil of Maipo Valley is noted for **HIGH SALINITY** from irrigation from the Maipo river.

Cabernet Sauvignon
Merlot
Carménère

95%

Sauvignon Blanc
Chardonnay

5%

Classifications

Key sub-regions within the Central Valley are Maipo (Alto Maipo, Central Maipo, and Pacific Maipo) Curicó, Rapel, and the Maule Valley.

Medium to high acidity and fruity style red wines. Often described as a blend between Bordeaux and California.

As its name suggests, the Central Valley is located in the middle of Chile. The Central Valley is home to four subregions: the Maipo Valley, the Maule Valley, the Curicó Valley, and the Rapel Valley. The Carménère grape, which is practically nonexistent in the vineyards of other countries, is the local star variety of the Central Valley. In this region, small-scale wines from the best combinations of terroirs and varieties are producing world-class wines.

Of these, the Maipo Valley is the most internationally recognized for its world-class Cabernet Sauvignon. This subregion helped establish Chile as a major wine-producing country, putting it on the map in the latter half of the twentieth century. The Maipo Valley is just south of the capital, Santiago, where several major wineries are based, and it is also the region in Chile which has the longest history of viticulture.

Like the Maipo Valley, the Rapel Valley also produces outstanding Cabernet Sauvignon, along with Carménère. It has since become the poster child for Chilean wine. The Curicó Valley is known for its Chardonnay and Sauvignon Blanc. As a cooler region, white wines thrive here.

The Central Valley enjoys a Mediterranean-like climate and distinct microclimate variations between individual regions and even subregions. With warm, dry summers and only thirty-eight to seventy-five centimeters (fifteen to thirty inches) of rainfall a year, Chile has a unique climate, supporting high-quality vines. Well-regarded labels in Chile include Concha y Toro, Emiliana, AlmaViva, ConoSur, and Los Vascos, to name a few.

Chile's Central Valley benefits from cooling influences coming off the Pacific Ocean courtesy of the Humboldt Current. This current provides maritime breezes and cooling fogs, which help preserve acidity in the grapes.

Recommend drinking bottles two to four years after the bottle date.

AUSTRALIA

Australia is the sixth largest wine-producing nation in the world and has a reputation for modern techniques, including canopy management and soil mapping. In a country geographically equal in size to the United States and all of Europe, the climate, soils and wines are diverse. Over the past several decades, Australia has been working to overcome a perception of lower quality export wines that dominated many of the bottom priced shelves at grocery stores.

Today, the star of Australian wine is Shiraz. What began as confusion to rename the Syrah grape from the Rhône Valley in France, marketing Shiraz allowed the industry's production to triple over the past thirty years. Following Shiraz, Cabernet Sauvignon and Chardonnay dwarf the plantings of the other several dozen grape varieties planted. Most of the wines from Australia are single-varietals, although blending, especially with Shiraz, is more common.

Stylistically, Australian wines tend to have higher alcohol, more prominent fruit flavors, oak aging for the reds and full-body, similar in style to a traditional wine from California. Some producers are harvesting their grapes earlier to constrain some of these elements and shifting to other grapes like Pinot Noir, Semillon and even Riesling. Select winemakers are also moving away from the intense oak aging and bold styles that are typical of Australian wines. Over the next decade I would expect that Australian wines will be fresher and more nuanced.

Australia generally tends to be extremely dry and irrigation is critical for the success of the vines. Humidity is extremely low and the combination of the mountains and the sea bring the perfect mixture to the vineyards in the south. The intense year-round sunshine makes southern Australia more suited to their traditional styles, despite some of the extreme variability the regions have experienced over the last decade.

Australian wine labels follow similar guidelines to other New World wines in that they focus on the grapes; however, Australia's regional classification system is extremely flexible. Quality standards exist that mandate at least eighty-five percent of the grapes used in production must come from a geographic area. This system is similar to the United States AVA and called the Geographical Indications (GI) System. This classification allows for the over 100 GI regions listed on the label to be as general or specific as desired. There are no restrictions on grape varieties or yields within the GIs.

The region listed on the label can be one of Australia's six states—New South Wales, Queensland, South Australia, Tasmania, Victoria, or Western Australia. However, the place listed can also be a zone, which is a smaller wine region within a state, a region (a smaller area within that zone), or a subregion (a designated area within the region). Alternatively, the location listed on the bottle can be as general as "Southeastern Australia," which is a massive geographic area.

Most of Australia's quality wine comes from the south: New South Wales, Victoria, and South Australia. In the Southeast there are a number of important regions to know. Since phylloxera has never troubled this area, Barossa Valley vines represent some of the oldest in the world and produce bold Shiraz. The Claire Valley and Eden Valley produces some excellent, fresh Rieslings. Coonawarra has a rich red soil and creates outstanding Cabernet Sauvignon wines. I had the opportunity to try a broad selection of Australian GI vintages that were ten years old, and I did not find them that pleasant to drink, so my recommendation is to drink Australian wines within a few years of their release date.

In Australia, you will find a lot of smaller producers, but those winemakers exist in the shadow of a highly industrialized and concentrated wine industry. In fact, four large companies represent eighty-five percent of the market. The concept of vintage, or terroir is much less important than the notion of brand and price. These large producers collect grapes that come from across the country and they are sourced for quality and price. The focus for the winemakers is not the expression of land, but exhibiting the taste of the fruit and achieving the correct levels of sweetness and alcohol.

Australian wines are primarily named for their grape variety. For the reds, Shiraz are typically medium to full-bodied wines with varying flavor profiles and structure depending on the winemaking techniques. Australian Cabernet Sauvignons are often dense, with notes of mint and herbs. Chardonnay is the most common white variety, with Semillon, Riesling and Sauvignon Blanc trailing. Chardonnay and Semillon are both typically full bodied, rich in alcohol and often marked by aromas of new wood and exotic fruits, although unoaked white wines are becoming more common. The Rieslings varietals are fruity but racy and Sauvignon Blanc wines often struggle to achieve higher acidity levels on their own.

AUSTRALIA: COONAWARRA

OUTSTANDING	EXCELLENT	VERY GOOD	GOOD	CHALLENGING
 2012 2013	 2001 2004 2005 2006 2015 2016	 2000 2009 2010 2014	 2002 2003 2007 2008	 2011

MARITIME CLIMATE with extensive cloud cover in summer that keeps the temperature down.

Cabernet Sauvignon
Shiraz
Grenache

90%

Chardonnay
Riesling
Sauvignon Blanc

10%

TERRA ROSSA SOIL over a thick layer of soft limestone.

Classifications

Five classifications exist within Australia from South-Eastern Australia, State of Origin, Zones, Regions, and Sub-Regions. The Langton's Classification system divides wine into three categories - Exceptional, Outstanding, and Excellent. Wynns Coonawarra Estate has been included on this list since 2014.

Firm tannin structure requires extended aging. Better wines are aged at least 18 months in oak prior to bottling.

Coonawarra is the Cabernet Sauvignon wine celebrity of Southern Australia's limestone coast. Located midway between Melbourne and Adelaide, its location is less popular among visitors due to the sheer distance from major cities. While its agricultural history began with raising sheep in the nineteenth century, the region now celebrates more than 120 years of winemaking.

Coonawarra's terroir forms the uniqueness of its wines. Coonawarra was frozen during the Ice Age, and when it thawed out, the region was under the sea and inhabited by marine life. When the water receded, it revealed a limestone foundation dusted with iron-rich clay soil. The region's vibrant red-orange earth takes the name of "terra rossa."

Coonawarra is only ninety-five kilometers (sixty miles) from the coast. Coonawarra vineyards enjoy a warm growing season, but cooling breezes and consistent cloud cover makes the region substantially cooler than you might expect. Winters are considered cold in Coonawarra.

Cabernet Sauvignon is the region's specialty—its distinct flavor is a blend of black and red fruits with savory tobacco. It ages gracefully in the bottle, much like Shiraz—the runner-up, with bold notes of pepper and minty herbs. Merlot, which is newer to the region, is also very good and expresses notes of cedar and plum. Coonawarra's red wine is typically medium- to full-bodied, deeply flavored with dark fruit, and has complexity from chewy tannins. You will recognize herbal and eucalyptus characters and a little spearmint. The wines have the potential to age well over decades. While Coonawarra also produces white wines, they make up less than ten percent of the region's total production.

Recommend drinking bottles six months to two years after the bottle date.

NEW ZEALAND

New Zealand may produce only one percent of the world's wines, but its geographical singularity makes it a region of note. The island's soil is largely volcanic. Its location in the Pacific Ocean, southeast of Australia, makes New Zealand the southernmost wine-producing country in the world. Not to mention, its vineyards are never further than 120 kilometers (seventy-five miles) from the coast.

White Sauvignon Blanc makes up seventy percent of the nation's wine production and is the signature wine of the country. Classically know as crisp with high acidity and a honeysuckle aroma, Sauvignon Blanc may be found across a large number of quality levels and price points on the islands. Pinot Noir plantings have also been rapidly expanding over the past decade and represent the second most planted varietal in New Zealand.

Their Geographical Indications (GI) system was just passed into law in 2016, and the wine industry has been rapidly evolving. There were fewer than one hundred New Zealand wineries thirty years ago, but today there are over 670. The GI identify eighteen distinct regions within New Zealand, and the focus is on producing wines with grapes from the identified region. Unlike the quality standards in France and Italy, in New Zealand, the GIs do not mandate vinification process, yields, or irrigation techniques.

New Zealand's wine industry is spread across the two islands: North Island and South Island. The smaller North Island is warmer, rainier, and less mountainous. Major wine regions on the North Island include Northland, Auckland, Waikato/Bay of Plenty, Gisborne, Hawkes Bay, and Wairarapa. South Island is divided by the Southern Alps protecting the vineyards from receiving too much precipitation. The major regions of the South Island are Nelson, Marlborough, Canterbury, and Central Otago.

For the most part, New Zealand wines follow common New World labelling. However, the local industry tends to follow more relaxed rules. For instance, the alcohol content is allowed a margin of error of 1.5 percent, which may seem low, but is three times higher than the EU allows for wines made there. Additionally, many bottles include the term "single vineyard," which means that every grape involved in production was grown on the same vineyard. Often, the name of the specific vineyard is included on the label.

The soils through New Zealand are dominated by clay. The cool, humid climate and water retaining properties of the clay can cause trouble in the vineyards as mold and rot can easily develop if not treated. This is in contrast to some of the other vineyards like Marlborough and Hawke's Bay where irrigation is needed since the Southern Alps block too much moisture from reaching the vines.

One word of caution when buying New Zealand brands: always check the back of the label before you purchase a bottle. Sometimes, New Zealand wineries will outsource to Australia and all wines produced in New Zealand should read "Wine of New Zealand" on the label in fine print. If it mentions Australia on the back, then eighty-five percent of the grapes involved in production did not originate from New Zealand at all.

Another important factor to consider when selecting New Zealand wine is the vintage listed on the label. Because New Zealand is a cool-climate growing region, variation from one year to the next is common depending on the weather conditions and the quality of the grape harvest that year.

New Zealand is also known for advancing the screwcap closure for wines. The desire for change has been championed by the New Zealand Screwcap Wine Seal Initiative setup in 2001. New Zealand producers were following the lead of Australian winemakers in the Clare Valley frustrated by cork-related faults. They argue that cork is inconsistent with regards to oxygen ingress and that synthetic closures were only suitable for wines destined to be consumed almost immediately. Inspired by this bold decision, producers in Marlborough, New Zealand undertook scientific research, the results of which drove them to the screwcaps. Then, one of the country's largest wine producers, Villa Maria, transitioned to screwcaps admiring a number of smaller producers that made the switch. In the years since the establishment of the New Zealand Screwcap Wine Seal Initiative, the number of screwcaps being used by wine producers on a global basis has increased dramatically. Eradicating cork taint, having no effect on the wine and forming a perfect seal, New Zealand winegrowers argue that this is an incredible achievement for the wine industry, particularly given the resistance from those in the market clinging to the tradition of cork. Despite these efforts, I think that the screwcap still has a stigma of association with low-quality, inexpensive wines for some buyers, but as we see new alternative packaging, like wine in a can, those sentiments may change. Some manufactures like Diam are producing sanitized natural cork products to eliminate impurities, so the movement to eliminate cork is still an open question.

NEW ZEALAND:
HAWKE'S BAY

OUTSTANDING	EXCELLENT	VERY GOOD	GOOD	CHALLENGING
2010 2013 2014 2016	2005 2006 2007 2009	2003 2004 2012	2001 2002 2008 2011 2015	2000

Maritime climate tempers **VERY SUNNY SUMMER DAYS**. Elevation offers some wind protection throughout the season.
Frost can damage vineyards inland.

Merlot
Cabernet Sauvignon
Syrah

50%

Chardonnay
Sauvignon Blanc
Pinot Gris

50%

Over twenty-five types of soils including alluvial **OVER GRAVELY SUB-SOILS** as well as sandy loams over clay.

Classifications

Coastal Areas, Hillsides, and Alluvial Plains are the three main sub-regions that exist within Hawke's Bay. River Valleys and Central Hawke's Bay also have distinct soil types and grape plantings. Both red and white grapes are often planted in these sub-regions.

Internationally known for high-quality Bordeaux-style red blends and full-bodied Chardonnays. Hawke's Bay has the highest percentage of Sustainable Winegrowing New Zealand (SWNZ) accredited wineries in the country.

Located along the North Island's east coast, Hawke's Bay is the best wine region in New Zealand. The climate is temperate and largely influenced by the Pacific Ocean and four major inland rivers that cut across it. The body of water for which the region is named, Hawke's Bay, is a semicircular bay just south of Gisborne. The viticulture region envelops Napier, Hastings, and Havelock North. The combination of the region's warm climate, long autumns, and naturally-occurring bodies of water make for rich soil that lends to great grapes. Not to mention, day-to-night temperature ranges make the region especially suited to winemaking.

Most of the region's soil is influenced by volcanic rock. This brings magnesium, calcium, sodium, iron, and potassium to the vines in a perfect balance of nutrients. Many vineyards also benefit from a mix of silt, clay, and gravel, as well.

Although Hawke's Bay is second to the Marlborough region in terms of production, it is New Zealand's leader in full-bodied reds, which make up eighty-eight percent of the country's total red wine production. Syrah wines from Hawke's Bay are perhaps the strongest in flavor, with notes of black pepper. However, some of the most successful wines from Hawke's Bay are blends—elegant Bordeaux blends in particular. Pinot Noir is another important wine here, with characteristics ranging across the region. Many have notes of cherries, berries, and flowers, while others tend to have more savory, rich flavors. The region's winemakers also create aromatic white wines, such as a fruity and full-bodied Chardonnay, as well as sweet dessert wines.

Recommend drinking bottles six months to two years after the bottle date.

NEW ZEALAND:
MARLBOROUGH

OUTSTANDING	EXCELLENT	VERY GOOD	GOOD	CHALLENGING
2005 2013	2003 2007 2009 2010 2016	2002 2006 2008 2011 2015	2000 2001 2012 2014	2004

Located on South Island, Marlborough is **COOL, DRY, AND SUNNY**. Protected from strong winds and rain from the Tasman Sea by the Southern Alps. Strong contrast between hot sunny days and cool nights.

 Pinot Noir

20%

 Sauvignon Blanc

80%

A mixture of clay and **WELL-DRAINING SOIL** throughout the region.

Classifications

Three sub-regions exist within Marlborough including the Southern Valleys, Wairau Valley, and the Awatere Valley.

Sauvignon Blanc is internationally recognized as one of the best expressions in the world. Unoaked Sauvignon Blancs are fermented in stainless steel or concrete vats and are known for their high acidity.

Marlborough produces most of the wine in New Zealand, but is best known for its sparkling wines and dry Sauvignon Blanc white wines. Marlborough's Sauvignon Blanc is distinct and quite strong, with grassy flavors of green pepper and gooseberry shining through each glass. The region is also home to enjoyable Pinot Noir wines that are notably light and fruity. These are categorized as cool-climate Pinot Noirs, due to the incredible terrain and weather that brings them from vine to bottle.

What makes Marlborough special is the diversity of soils. Close to the major rivers in the Wairau Plains, the soils range from stony former riverbed gravels to deep fertile silt. Further south in the Awatere Valley, loess and mixed stony gravel can be found. It is not uncommon to see a variety of three different soil types within a small vineyard.

The region can be divided into two major zones, separated by the Wither Hills. One subregion is the Wairau Valley which has two distinct terrains: the low-lying banks of the Wairu River, and the southern hills closer to Brancott and Omaka. The Wairau Valley receives very little rainfall. In fact, the native Maori people once called the area "the place with the hole in the cloud," because they rarely saw an overcast day.

Southeast of the Wairau Valley sits the Awatere Valley, which is the second major subregion of Marlborough. It is closer to the Pacific Ocean and receives more sea breezes that keep the temperatures cooler and raises the acidity level in the wines. Vines here grow on the terraced riverbanks.

Recommend drinking bottles one to three years after the bottle date.

SOUTH AFRICA

South African viticulture began in the mid-1600s as Dutch colonists stopped in Cape Town during their voyages around the southern African continent. The next four-hundred years, however, were challenging as new trade routes, phylloxera, other vine disease and trade restrictions from apartheid greatly restricted the wine export market. South Africa's wine industry, like many other new world examples, is less than thirty years old.

Cool ocean breezes, called the Benguela Current, brings fog and moderating temperatures to the warm vineyards producing ideal conditions for grape growing, especially in the southwest. The constant air flow reduces the risk of mildew on the vines while maintaining an ideal temperature for the grapes. This, combined with some of the oldest soils in the world create a rich environment for vineyards.

South Africa's wine-producing regions are divided into five geographical areas: Western Cape, Northern Cape, Eastern Cape, KwaZulu-Natal, and Limpopo. Within the Northern Cape there are five production areas: the Douglas and Sutherland-Karoo districts, and the Hartswater, Central Orange River, and Rietrivier FS wards. The Eastern Cape has a single ward: St. Francis Bay. Kwazulu-Natal and Limpopo do not have any specific production areas. Most South African wine production occurs in the Western Cape, including Stellenbosch and Paarl. Historically, the sweet wine region of Constantia was the best known wine in South Africa, but as global tastes changed, the success of the Sauvignon Blanc white wine have faded.

Today, South Africa's most widely-planted and best-quality grape is Chenin Blanc, sometimes called "Steen." You will find just about every possible style of Chenin Blanc from light and fresh to full-body oaked varieties. You will also see dessert wines, including botrytis-affected grapes adding sweet honey flavors to the wine. Some other whites like Chardonnay, Sauvignon Blanc, and Colombard are also grown, mostly creating dry whites. Over the past thirty years, red grapes became more common as well. Cabernet Sauvignon, Shiraz and the signature Pinotage grape produce generally dark red, full-bodied wines with a lot of fruit expression.

South African wine labels are fairly straightforward. The first thing listed will be an appellation from one of the country's regions. After the location, the label will list the grape variety and vintage, the name of the producer, and the alcohol content. When a blend consists of two grapes, the rules mandate that they must be listed in order of quantity.

South African wines can carry one of two seals: The Wine of Origin seal (WO) or Integrated Production of Wine (IPW), combined. The Wine of Origin system was developed in 1973 and sets basic rules for South African wineries. Here, the South African Wine Industry Information and Systems (SAWIS) verifies the quality. To receive this seal, the designated region must supply one hundred percent of the grapes involved in production. Two-thirds must originate from one vintage and must originate from a single variety of grape. If a single grape variety is listed on the label, then a minimum of seventy-five percent of the wine must comprise the specified grape if the wine is sold domestically, and eighty-five percent if exported.

The IPW designation focuses on sustainability. Organic and biodynamic vineyards are on the rise in South Africa, and the IPW sets guidelines for agricultural, manufacturing, and packaging practices. To receive this seal, winemakers must follow the Global Wine Sector Environmental Sustainability Principles. However, you won't find seals or labels that highlight IPW certification alone. Because there is no option for an IPW seal, IPW wines must also comply with WO rules to receive a joint seal that highlights both statuses.

Over the next decade, one of the greatest challenges for the South African wine industry will be water. Several years of drought in the Western Cape has severely impacted yield levels as water quotas are reduced and the vines struggle to keep up production. Water restrictions will not only decrease the volume of wine produced but also increase costs in years to come. Irrigation causes the roots to stay closer to the surface and be more vulnerable in drought years. Expect entry-level wines to become more expensive as stocks are diminished and the drought continues. This will strain even the larger wine makers. On the positive side, lower yields and smaller grapes make for more concentrated and perhaps better-quality wines. Farming and production costs will, however, continue to increase the prices for premium wines. With relatively small volumes of South Africa's top wines, demand will be greater than the supply.

SOUTH AFRICA:
STELLENBOSCH

OUTSTANDING	EXCELLENT	VERY GOOD	GOOD	CHALLENGING
2003 2009	2000 2001 2006 2015	2002 2005 2007 2012	2004 2008 2011 2013 2014 2016	2010

Relatively **HOT AND DRY** with some maritime influence resulting from winds from the Bengela Current from Antarctica.

Granite and **SANDSTONE SOILS**.

Pinotage
Cabernet Sauvignon
Syrah
Merlot
Pinot Noir

60%

Chenin Blanc / Steen
Chardonnay
Sauvignon Blanc

40%

Classifications

For vintage years, 85% of the grapes must be from that year, and the same percentage for varietals used. There are four levels of geographic designation from Regions and Districts to Wards and Estates.

Bodeaux style blends with Cabernet Sauvignon and Merlot aged in oak. Some producers create a port-style and sherry-style.

The star of South African wines regions, Stellenbosch is not far from Cape Town. Stellenbosch's Cabernet Sauvignon red wines are the best that you will find in the country. Wards located within Stellenbosch include Devon Valley, Jonkershoek Valley, Papegaaiberg, Simonsberg-Stellenbosch, Bottelary, Banghoek, and the Polkadraai Hills.

South Africa's wide-ranging soils that include decomposed granite and sandstone on the hillsides, combined with the warm and sunny climate, produce outstanding Cabernet Sauvignon and Sauvignon Blanc wines. Merlot, Shiraz, and Chenin Blanc are also of very high quality in the region.

The best wineries create full-bodied, wood-matured red wines with densely opaque colors. The wines have flavors of black fruit and sweet plums, with a smooth mouthfeel and elements of cedar oak spice. Some of the more interesting bottles have moist fruit cake flavors with nuances of cinnamon spice.

Trying the individual producers is important in Stellenbosch as winemakers have a lot of choices in vinification. A typical process in Stellenbosch involves de-stemming, crushing, and then pumping into open tanks. This mixture of grape skins and juice is combined for several days. Non-native yeast strains are used, and fermentation occurs for about a week. The wine is then left on the skins for another month before separation. Malolactic fermentation is done in the tank and then aged in oak for over a year.

If you have the opportunity to visit Stellenbosch, the South African wine industry has created several Wine Routes. These wine routes comprise of a network of over 150 wineries divided by geography and climate to provide an immersive experience to enjoy their wines.

Recommend drinking bottles one to four years after the bottle date.

SOUTH AFRICA:
PAARL

OUTSTANDING	EXCELLENT	VERY GOOD	GOOD	CHALLENGING
2000 2003 2009	2001 2006 2007	2004 2005 2008 2012	2011 2013 2014 2015 2016	2002 2010

Relatively hot compared to the more coastal areas of the Western Cape. **LONG SUMMERS AND COLD, RAINY WINTERS** are typical. Rainfall is moderate to high.

Shiraz
Pinotage
Cabernet Sauvignon

80%

Chenin Blanc (Steen)
Chardonnay
Viognier

20%

GRANITE AND SANDY soils throughout the region.

Classifications

Following the WO system, there are some stellar single estates that produce top quality Shiraz and Pinotage wines with the districts of Wellington and Franschhoek leading the way.

Expressive and fruity reds resulting in wines with depth and complexity.

Not far from Cape Town, Paarl was South Africa's third European settlement, located just sixty kilometers (thirty-eight miles) inland in the Cape Winelands region of the Western Cape. This region is incredibly diverse and creates a lot of high-quality varieties. While dry Cabernet Sauvignon, Shiraz, Pinotage, Chenin Blanc, and Chardonnay are all excellent here, the winemakers also produce botrytised and fortified dessert wines.

Shiraz, Pinotage, and Cabernet Sauvignon tend to be rich and fruity. Chardonnay and Chenin Blanc grapes are used to create white wines that have a light tropical fruit taste. The most successful of these varieties tend to come from two of Paarl's subregions: Wellington and Voor Paardeberg. Wellington benefits from its proximity to the Berge and Kromme Rivers. In Wellington, mountain shadows reduce sun exposure, allowing the grapes to ripen more gradually and ultimately develop more acidity and

greater flavors. Pinotage and Chenin Blanc are the subregion's most successful wines. The other subregion, Voor Paardeberg, has a slightly different soil than the rest of Paarl. It is composed almost entirely of granite and is rich in potassium, which strengthens the vines. Voor Paardeberg produces noteworthy Shiraz, which is fruity and spicy.

Geographically, Paarl's borders include Wellington in the northwest and several mountain ranges in the southeast. The Boland Mountains mark the region's east, while Paarl Rock marks the west—the latter being the granite rock for which the region is named. While vines situated on the eastern slopes of the Berg River receive plenty of water, vines rooted elsewhere benefit from irrigation. Summers are long and hot, while winters are cooler with heavy rainfalls.

Recommend drinking bottles six months to three years after the bottle date.

FINAL THOUGHTS

I find wine fascinating, as it is a bit of a paradox. Fundamentally, a wine grower is a farmer. They grow grapes. In modern farming, tools that help growers measure moisture content, sugar levels, and acidity and predict upcoming weather events are critical to producing the best-quality grapes.

After harvest, the chemistry of winemaking begins. Fermentation occurs through several biochemical steps under a blanket of carbon dioxide, where the phenols in the juice are oxidized and the sugar and ethanol are converted to carbon dioxide and water. Winemaking is chemistry. Visiting the winemakers, they reminded me of laboratories where scientists are working to produce the best possible wine.

Science, however, is not enough to produce great wines. The art form of wine production: knowing the vines and the terroir, caring for the grapes, and crafting blends to extract the very best flavors is the essence of winemaking. Even in regions with strict quality guidelines, the best winemakers show creativity and genius in their bottles not by following a recipe and a process but understanding when to deviate from those methods to achieve the greatest wine. A lot of winemakers spoke about their failures, and how those failures formed their understanding of the wine and led to their future success. Failure is a big part of winemaking.

While this project started with a lot of data analysis, the most impactful experiences that I had was meeting with the individual wine producers in the regions, hearing their approaches and stories to winemaking, and trying their wines in the region. Especially in areas where generational winemakers care for family-run wineries, it is not about the business of wine, but the passion for winemaking that drives the success of the industry. Wine is about creating connections—connections to people, food, villages, experiences, and terroir.

So while data, metrics, and science are important and can provide critical tools to understand wine, the journey to discover great wines can't stop there. In fact, the journey to find the great wines of the world will never end. The more you learn about the wine and the people producing it, the more you will realize how little you actually understand. That is the great thing about wine. It's the journey and the exploration of the fruit, people, and regions that make wine a passion. There never is an end—just another beginning.

SELECTED BIBLIOGRAPHY

I list here only the writings and sources that have been of use in the making of this book. This bibliography is by no means a complete record of all of the works and resources that I have consulted. It indicates the substance and range of reading upon which I have formed by ideas and is a resource for those who wish to learn more about the wine regions.

Gibson, Michael, *The Sommelier Prep Course*, Hoboken: John Wiley & Sons, 2010.

Herbst, Ron, Sharon Tyler Herbst, *The New Wine Lover's Companion* Fourth Edition, New York: Barron's Educational Series, 2017.

Liem, Peter, *Champagne*, New York: Ten Speed Press, 2017.

Norman, Remmington, *Grand Cru*, New York: Sterling Epicure, 2011.

MacNeil, Karen, *The Wine Bible*, New York: Workman Publishing, 2015.

Puckette, Madeline, Justin Hammack, *The Essential Guide to Wine*, New York: Avery, 2015.

The website of GuildSomm, www.guildsomm.com.

The website of Italian Wine Central, www.italianwinecentral.com.

The website of the Wine Scholar Guild, www.winescholarguild.org.

The website of Wine and Spirit Education Trust, www.wsetglobal.com.

APPENDIX

I wanted to write a book about wine, not statistical analysis and data processing. I do think that it is important, however, to show how I came to the results in the book, so this appendix illustrates at least the result of the analysis I performed for this project. While you may agree or disagree with my approach, I hope it opens the discussion on different ways to select the best wines. I'm not a data scientist or mathematician, but with the large amount of data accessible in a wide range of areas, it is possible to synthesize and normalize it to produce some interesting findings.

These 197 wine regions are not a comprehensive listing of every wine region in the world. Nor may they be compared equally, as we discussed earlier in the book. Wine regions in some countries, districts, or states are more granular than others, so this is not a perfect science.

I selected four summary categories: Composite Vintage Score, Weather and Climate, Producer Quality & Controls, and Sensory Evaluation for the period 2000-2016. The total maximum score of these four areas could equal 100 points.

For the Composite Vintage Score, I examined each year and assigned from zero-three points for that vintage based on several factors. These factors included an average of professional review scores for producers within the region, and consumer reviews and comments on producers within that region. You may find the more detailed results of the vintage data within the infographics throughout the book. This crowdsourced data was the most heavily weighted for the book, although it is a disadvantage for lesser known regions or for regions with fewer producers.

The Weather and Climate variables evaluated the conditions from 2000-2016, and variance from the typical yield usually based on extreme weather events. Recorded challenges with temperature, frost, hail, precipitation, wind, and other vine-affecting factors detracted from the score in this area. Typical years were assigned a single point for each year that were within 80% of the average weather for that season.

Producer Quality & Controls looked at both the larger quality systems that were developed at the county or regional level, as well as unique standards and processes that local producers followed within the area. These may include aging requirements, restrictions on yields, chaptalization, acidification, grape varietal controls, or other production standards.

The last category was the most subjective, Sensory Evaluation. I tasted one-five of the examples of the wine from the region if available. It was weighted the least not just because of the subjectivity, but as many of the lesser known regions were extremely difficult to find, so tasting more than a single producer was not possible for wines after the top 100. More importantly, why would I write a book about wine, while not tasting the wine and factoring that into the score.

For the total numeric score, I set 50 points as the minimum for inclusion in the book. Because of the variability in the data, limited information for the lesser known regions and subjectivity of the normalization, I choose not to organize the book as the "Top X Wine Regions" in order of rankings. Instead, I thought that it was more compelling to arrange them in the book by country, and include this appendix for those who are interesting in seeing the data behind the pages.

	Composite Vintage Score 2000-2016	Weather and Climate 2000-2016	Producer Quality & Controls 2000-2016	Sensory Evaluation 2000-2016	TOTAL POINTS
MAXIMUM SCORE	48	16	32	4	100
France: Burgundy	47	12	22	4	85
Italy: Piedmont	45	13	22	4	84
Spain: Priorat	46	12	22	4	84
France: Alsace	42	12	24	4	82
France: Champagne	45	10	23	4	82
France: Bordeaux	47	10	20	4	81
Spain: Rioja	43	12	22	4	81
United States: North Coast	46	13	18	4	81
Italy: Veneto	41	12	21	4	78
France: Rhône Valley	40	13	20	4	77
France: Loire Valley	43	10	19	4	76
Italy: Friuli-Venezia Giulia	39	14	20	3	76
Italy: Tuscany	46	11	15	4	76
Germany: Rheinhessen	44	11	16	4	75
Portugal: Vinho Verde	41	12	19	3	75
Germany: Mosel	43	11	16	4	74
Spain: Penedès	35	14	20	4	73
Germany: Rheingau	42	11	16	3	72
Spain: Rías Baixas	40	8	19	4	71
Germany: Pfalz	41	10	15	4	70

	Composite Vintage Score 2000-2016	Weather and Climate 2000-2016	Producer Quality & Controls 2000-2016	Sensory Evaluation 2000-2016	TOTAL POINTS
France: Provence	34	14	18	3	69
Spain: Ribera del Duero	34	12	19	4	69
Italy: Trentino-Alto Adige	37	8	20	3	68
New Zealand: Marlborough	41	13	10	4	68
Austria: Wachau	33	10	20	4	67
Portugal: Douro Valley	37	9	17	3	66
Italy: Marche	35	8	19	3	65
Italy: Sicily	32	14	16	3	65
Italy: Emilia-Romagna	32	9	20	3	64
United States: Columbia Valley	39	10	12	3	64
Italy: Lombardy	33	9	18	3	63
United States: Finger Lakes	35	12	11	3	61
Austria: Kamptal	31	9	15	3	58
United States: Willamette Valley	31	11	13	3	58
Australia: Coonawarra	35	7	12	3	57
Austria: Kremstal	30	9	15	3	57
South Africa: Stellenbosch	31	13	10	3	57
Argentina: Mendoza	39	5	9	3	56
New Zealand: Hawke's Bay	31	12	10	3	56
South Africa: Paarl	30	13	10	3	56
Argentina: Salta	38	4	9	3	54
United States: Middleburg	28	11	10	3	52
Chile: Central Valley	32	6	9	3	50
France: Languedoc-Roussillon	13	13	18	4	48
France: Beaujolais	15	9	20	3	47
Australia: McLaren Vale	21	13	9	3	46
Australia: Riverland	20	14	9	3	46
France: Corsica	11	12	20	3	46
France: Jura	12	11	20	3	46
United States: Columbia Valley	21	13	9	3	46
France: Savoie	12	10	20	3	45
United States: Central Coast	20	12	10	3	45
Australia: Yarra Valley	19	13	9	3	44
Spain: Jerez	23	10	8	3	44

	Composite Vintage Score 2000-2016	Weather and Climate 2000-2016	Producer Quality & Controls 2000-2016	Sensory Evaluation 2000-2016	TOTAL POINTS
Australia: Hunter	19	12	9	3	43
Australia: Robe	19	12	9	3	43
Australia: Tasmania	18	12	9	3	42
Germany: Mittelrhein	17	12	10	3	42
New Zealand: Central Otago	19	10	10	3	42
New Zealand: Waikato	17	12	10	3	42
United States: Monticello	18	13	8	3	42
Australia: Barossa Valley	20	9	9	3	41
Australia: Eden Valley	19	10	9	3	41
Austria: Wagram	13	10	16	2	41
New Zealand: Auckland	18	10	10	3	41
New Zealand: Waitaki Valley	16	12	10	3	41
Portugal: Dão	20	9	9	3	41
United States: Sierra Foothills	16	13	8	4	41
Australia: Riverina	18	10	9	3	40
Austria: Carnuntum	12	9	18	1	40
Austria: Neusiedlersee	17	10	10	3	40
Chile: Atacama	19	11	7	3	40
Germany: Ahr	15	12	10	3	40
Germany: Baden	16	11	10	3	40
Germany: Franken	17	10	10	3	40
Hungry: Tokaji Aszú	16	11	10	3	40
New Zealand: Northland	16	11	10	3	40
Portugal: Alentejano	17	10	10	3	40
Portugal: Madeira	23	6	7	4	40
Spain: Rueda	22	9	5	4	40
Germany: Nahe	15	11	10	3	39
New Zealand: Gisborne	17	10	10	2	39
Portugal: Península de Setúbal	20	8	8	3	39
Spain: Costers del Segre	18	12	7	2	39
Spain: Tarragona	19	11	6	3	39
Australia: Adelaide Hills	13	14	9	2	38
Chile: Coquimbo	18	11	7	2	38
Germany: Hessische Bergstrasse	13	13	10	2	38
Germany: Württemberg	15	12	9	2	38

	Composite Vintage Score 2000-2016	Weather and Climate 2000-2016	Producer Quality & Controls 2000-2016	Sensory Evaluation 2000-2016	TOTAL POINTS
Spain: Aragón	19	9	8	2	38
Spain: Murcia	19	10	7	2	38
New Zealand: Canterbury	15	10	10	2	37
New Zealand: Nelson	14	11	10	2	37
Portugal: Bairrada	19	6	10	2	37
Portugal: Beira Atlântico	19	9	7	2	37
South Africa: Walker Bay	19	7	9	2	37
Spain: Cigales	19	9	7	2	37
Spain: Navarra	18	10	7	2	37
Switzerland: Vaud	14	12	8	3	37
Austria: Leithaberg	14	10	10	2	36
Germany: Saale-Unstrut	14	10	10	2	36
Italy: Basilicata	17	9	8	2	36
Portugal: Algarve	19	9	6	2	36
Germany: Sachsen	13	11	9	2	35
Italy: Abruzzo	18	8	6	3	35
Italy: Sardinia	18	8	7	2	35
Portugal: Tejo	17	7	9	2	35
South Africa: Cape Town	16	7	9	3	35
South Africa: Swartland	16	8	9	2	35
United States: South Coast	14	10	9	2	35
Argentina: San Juan	15	10	7	2	34
Australia: Gundagai	12	11	9	2	34
Austria: Mittelburgenland	15	8	8	3	34
Austria: Traisental	15	9	8	2	34
Greece: Nemea	12	10	10	2	34
South Africa: Darling	14	9	9	2	34
United States: San Francisco Bay	14	10	8	2	34
Argentina: Tucumán	14	10	7	2	33
Australia: Orange	11	11	9	2	33
Austria: Weinviertel	12	10	9	2	33
Chile: Aconcagua	13	10	7	3	33
Greece: Patras	11	10	10	2	33
Greece: Peloponnese	11	10	10	2	33
Italy: Puglia	17	7	7	2	33
Slovakia: Moravia	8	9	15	1	33
South Africa: Elgin	13	9	9	2	33
Spain: Castilla-La-Mancha	17	7	7	2	33
Spain: Montsant	14	8	9	2	33

	Composite Vintage Score 2000-2016	Weather and Climate 2000-2016	Producer Quality & Controls 2000-2016	Sensory Evaluation 2000-2016	TOTAL POINTS
Switzerland: Lake Geneva	13	10	8	2	33
Switzerland: Valais	12	11	8	2	33
Argentina: La Pampa	12	10	7	3	32
Australia: Currency Creek	12	9	9	2	32
Australia: Southern Flinders Ranges	14	7	9	2	32
Austria: Eisenberg	12	9	9	2	32
Austria: Schilcherland	11	10	9	2	32
Austria: Weiner Gemischter Satz	11	9	10	2	32
Greece: Macedonia	9	11	10	2	32
Isreal: Shomron	10	12	8	2	32
Italy: Campania	19	6	5	2	32
Argentina: Catamarca	13	9	7	2	31
Chile: Austral Region	13	9	7	2	31
Hungry: Eszencia	10	10	9	2	31
Israel: Galilee	9	12	8	2	31
Isreal: Negev	9	12	8	2	31
Italy: Umbria	15	8	6	2	31
Argentina: Río Negro	12	9	7	2	30
Australia: Perth Hills	9	10	9	2	30
Croatia: Primorska Hrvatska	8	10	10	2	30
Romania: Banatului	11	8	9	2	30
Romania: Crisanei si Maramuresului	11	9	9	1	30
South Africa: Cape Agulhas	11	8	9	2	30
Croatia: Kontinentalna Hrvatska	9	9	9	2	29
Italy: Lazio	16	6	6	1	29
South Africa: Overberg	10	9	9	1	29
Argentina: Neuquén	11	9	7	1	28
Chile: Southern Regions	10	10	7	1	28
Georgia: Kakheti	10	9	8	1	28
Greece: Aegean Islands	8	9	10	1	28
Isreal: Shimshon	7	12	8	1	28
Mexico: Zacatecas	9	10	8	1	28
Romania: Podisului Transilvaniei	9	9	9	1	28
Romania: Teraselor Dunarii	9	9	9	1	28
South Africa: Calitzdorp	9	9	9	1	28

	Composite Vintage Score 2000-2016	Weather and Climate 2000-2016	Producer Quality & Controls 2000-2016	Sensory Evaluation 2000-2016	TOTAL POINTS
South Africa: Ceres Plateau	10	8	9	1	28
South Africa: Sutherland-Karoo	11	7	9	1	28
South Africa: Worcester	10	8	9	1	28
China: Ningxia	7	9	10	1	27
England: East Malling	9	7	9	2	27
Isreal: Jerusalem Mountains	6	12	8	1	27
Romania: Dealurilor Moldovei	8	9	9	1	27
Slovenia: Primorska	9	8	9	1	27
South Africa: Breeddekloof	9	8	9	1	27
South Africa: Plettenberg	9	8	9	1	27
Armenia: Ararat Valley	8	9	8	1	26
Canada: Ontario	9	8	8	1	26
China: Shandong	9	10	6	1	26
Georgia: Black Sea Coast	8	9	8	1	26
Georgia: Racha-Lechkhumi	8	9	8	1	26
Lebanon: Bekaa Valley	8	10	7	1	26
Mexico: Querétaro	8	9	8	1	26
Mexico: Sonora	9	8	8	1	26
Slovenia: Podravje	8	8	9	1	26
South Africa: Citrusdal Mountain	8	8	9	1	26
South Africa: Douglas	9	7	9	1	26
Ukraine: Simferopol	12	9	4	1	26
Bulgaria: Danubian Plain	7	10	7	1	25
Bulgaria: Thracian Lowlands	7	10	7	1	25
China: Xinjiang	8	10	6	1	25
Mexico: Hidalgo	7	9	8	1	25
Romania: Colinelor Dobrogei	7	8	9	1	25
Romania: Dealurilor Munteniei si Olteniei	6	9	9	1	25
South Africa: Robertson	8	7	9	1	25
Brazil: São Paulo	7	9	7	1	24
China: Yunnan	9	8	6	1	24

INDEX

ABOUT THE AUTHOR

Michael Biddick is a traveling sommelier who uses his background in technology to discover the world's best bottles of wine. A French Wine Scholar (FSW), and former contributing technology editor at *InformationWeek* and *Network Computing* magazines, Biddick uses accessible analytics to help people professionally understand wine culture. Biddick founded one of the fastest growing information technology firms in the country in 2009 and earned a Master of Science in Information Systems from Johns Hopkins University. Biddick speaks English, Spanish, and French and currently lives outside Washington, D.C.